MW00824019

Legal Notice

\

BOOKS FROM THE GET 800 COLLECTION
FOR COLLEGE BOUND STUDENTS

The Scholarly Unicorn's SAT Math Advanced Guide
28 SAT Math Lessons to Improve Your Score in One Month
> Beginner Course
> Intermediate Course
> Advanced Course

New SAT Math Problems arranged by Topic and Difficulty Level
320 SAT Math Problems arranged by Topic and Difficulty Level
SAT Verbal Prep Book for Reading and Writing Mastery
320 SAT Math Subject Test Problems
> Level 1 Test
> Level 2 Test

320 SAT Chemistry Subject Test Problems
Vocabulary Builder
28 ACT Math Lessons to Improve Your Score in One Month
> Beginner Course
> Intermediate Course
> Advanced Course

320 ACT Math Problems arranged by Topic and Difficulty Level
320 GRE Math Problems arranged by Topic and Difficulty Level
320 AP Calculus AB Problems
320 AP Calculus BC Problems
Physics Mastery for Advanced High School Students
400 SAT Physics Subject Test and AP Physics Problems
SHSAT Verbal Prep Book to Improve Your Score in Two Months
555 Math IQ Questions for Middle School Students
555 Advanced Math Problems for Middle School Students
555 Geometry Problems for High School Students
Algebra Handbook for Gifted Middle School Students
1000 Logic and Reasoning Questions for Gifted and Talented
> Elementary School Students

CONNECT WITH DR. STEVE WARNER

www.facebook.com/SATPrepGet800

www.youtube.com/TheSATMathPrep

www.twitter.com/SATPrepGet800

www.linkedin.com/in/DrSteveWarner

www.pinterest.com/SATPrepGet800

plus.google.com/+SteveWarnerPhD

The Scholarly Unicorn's
SAT Math Question Bank

Student Workbook with 1000 Problems

Dr. Steve Warner

Table of Contents

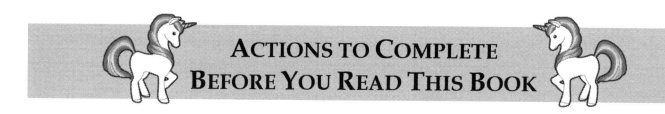

1. Purchase a TI-84 or equivalent calculator

It is recommended that you use a TI-84 or comparable calculator for the SAT. Answer explanations (available for free download – see 3 below) will always assume you are using such a calculator.

2. Take a practice SAT from the Official Guide to get your preliminary SAT math score

You can use the Get 800 Diagnostic Math Test (see 3 below), your last PSAT/SAT math score, or an official College Board practice SAT for this. Use this score to help you determine the problems you should be focusing on. Students scoring below 500 should work on only Level 1, 2, and 3 problems. Students scoring between 500 and 600 should work on Level 1, 2, 3, and 4 problems. Students scoring above 600 should work on all problems.

3. Claim your FREE bonuses

See page 248 for details on how to receive solutions to all the problems in this book and other materials, including a diagnostic SAT math test and 2 SAT math practice tests.

4. 'Like' my Facebook page

This page is updated regularly with SAT prep advice, tips, tricks, strategies, and practice problems. Visit the following webpage and click the 'like' button.

www.facebook.com/SATPrepGet800

LESSON 1 – HEART OF ALGEBRA
SOLVING LINEAR EQUATIONS

Full solutions to all problems in this book are available for free download. See page 248 for details. Problems marked with an asterisk (*) require a calculator.

LEVEL 1

1. If $5 + x + x = 1 + x + x + x$, what is the value of x ?

   A) 1
   B) 2
   C) 3
   D) 4

$$x + x + 6x - 6 = 5 + 4 + 2x + x + x + x$$

2. In the equation above, what is the value of x ?

   A) 5
   B) $\frac{15}{4}$
   C) $-\frac{2}{3}$
   D) -5

3. If $2j = \frac{x-4}{3}$ and $j = 6$, what is the value of x ?

   A) 10
   B) 20
   C) 30
   D) 40

4. For what value of x is $\frac{5x}{2} - 7 = 23$?

$$\frac{3}{7}x = \frac{4}{3}$$

5. What value of x is the solution of the equation above?

   A) $\frac{4}{7}$
   B) $\frac{9}{7}$
   C) $\frac{28}{9}$
   D) $\frac{28}{3}$

LEVEL 2

$$L = 11 + 1.6M$$

6. One end of an elastic band is taped to the bottom of a ceiling fan. When an object of mass M kilograms is attached to the other end of the elastic band, the band stretches to a length of L centimeters as shown in the equation above. What is M when $L = 13$?

7. If $4x - 5 = 53$, what is the value of $12x - 2$?

LEVEL 3

8. If $15x = 73$, what is the value of $3(x + \frac{4}{5})$?

   A) 17
   B) 15
   C) $\frac{73}{15}$
   D) $\frac{77}{15}$

9. On Sunday, Janice studied 3 more hours than Chris. If they studied for a combined total of 13 hours, how many hours did Chris study for on Sunday?

   A) 5
   B) 6
   C) 7
   D) 8

LEVEL 4

10. A gymnast's final score is determined by the sum of the difficulty score and execution score, less any deductions for neutral errors. Jackie had a difficulty score of p points and an execution score of q points. Assuming that Jackie lost $\frac{1}{8}$ of a point for each of her 20 neutral errors and had a final score of 6.5, what is the value of $p + q$?

LESSON 2 – PASSPORT TO ADVANCED MATH
FACTORING

LEVEL 1

1. Which of the following is equivalent to the expression $35b + 40bk$?

   A) $(7 + 8k)b$
   B) $(35 + 40k)b$
   C) $75(b + 2k)$
   D) $75b^2k$

$$7x(y + 4z)$$

2. Which of the following is equivalent to the expression above?

   A) $xy + 11xz$
   B) $7xy + 11xz$
   C) $7xy + 4z$
   D) $7xy + 28xz$

LEVEL 2

$$3x^2 - 7 = (ax + b)(ax - b)$$

3. In the equation above, a and b are constants. Which of the following could be the value of a ?

   A) 1.5
   B) $\sqrt{3}$
   C) 3
   D) 9

4. The length of a rectangular garden is k meters, and the width of the garden is 10 meters longer than its length. Which of the following expresses the area, in meters, of the garden in terms of k ?

   A) $2k + 10$
   B) $4k + 20$
   C) $k^2 + 10$
   D) $k^2 + 10k$

LEVEL 3

$$4x^4 + 16x^2y^2 + 16y^4$$

5. Which of the following is equivalent to the expression shown above?

   A) $(2x + 4y)^4$
   B) $(2x^2 + 4y^2)^2$
   C) $(4x + 16y)^4$
   D) $(4x^2 + 16y^2)^2$

6. Which of the following is equivalent to the expression $x^3y + x^2y^3 + 3x + 3y^2$?

A) $x^2y(x+1) + 3x(x+y^2)$
B) $(xy+3)(x^2+y^2)$
C) $(x^2y+3)(x+y^2)$
D) $x^2y(x+3+y)$

$$7(a+b) = 2(b-a)$$

7. If (a,b) is a solution to the equation above and $a \neq 0$, what is the ratio $\frac{b}{a}$?

A) $-\frac{9}{5}$
B) $-\frac{8}{5}$
C) 8
D) 11

8. Which of the following is equivalent to $(\frac{ab}{c})(cb - a)$?

A) $ab^2 - \frac{b}{c}$
B) $ab^2 - \frac{a^2b}{c}$
C) $\frac{ab}{c} - \frac{a^2b}{c}$
D) $\frac{ab}{c} - a^2bc$

LEVEL 4

9. If $x - y = \frac{27}{2}$ and $x + y = \frac{4}{9}$, what is the value of $x^2 - y^2$?

10. Let $m = 2x + 7$ and $k = 2x - 7$, and write $km = cx^2 + d$, where c and d are constants. What is the value of $c - d$?

LESSON 3 – PROBLEM SOLVING
RATIOS

LEVEL 1

1. At an adoption center, 4 guinea pigs are selected at random from each group of 15. At this rate, how many guinea pigs will be selected in total if the adoption center has 90 guinea pigs?

2. * In a random sample of 125 light bulbs, 4 are found to be broken. At this rate, how many of 9,750 light bulbs will be broken?

   A) 250
   B) 268
   C) 300
   D) 312

3. * The sculpture *Winged Victory of Samothrace* stands 5.57 meters high and has an approximate width of 1.524 meters. If a duplicate of the sculpture is made where each dimension is $\frac{1}{7}$ the corresponding original dimension, what is the height of the duplicate to the nearest tenth of a meter?

LEVEL 2

4. * The tallest giraffe on record was a male that stood 19.3 feet tall. Approximately what is the height of the tallest giraffe on record in <u>meters</u>? (1 meter ≈ 3.28 feet)

   A) 0.17
   B) 2.79
   C) 5.88
   D) 63.3

5. If a standard pallet can carry 60 boxes, then how many boxes can p pallets carry?

   A) $p + 60$
   B) $\frac{60}{p}$
   C) $\frac{p}{60}$
   D) $60p$

6. * Running at a constant speed, a race horse traveled 205 meters in 8.2 seconds. At this rate, what is the distance, in meters, the horse will travel in 2 minutes?

LEVEL 3

1 hectometer = 100 meters

10 decimeters = 1 meter

7. A manager splits his warehouse into equal subdivisions so that each subdivision has a length of 3 hectometers. Based on the information given above, what is the length, in decimeters, of each subdivison of the warehouse?

A) 30,000
B) 3,000
C) 30
D) 0.003

8. * Dennis completed a 1600 meter race in 145 seconds. What was his average speed, to the nearest meter, in meters per <u>minute</u>?

LEVEL 4

9. Starting from rest, a cat begins chasing a mouse, traveling d feet in t seconds. For the first ten seconds of the chase, the distance d can be estimated by using the formula $d = 9t^2\sqrt{t}$. Which of the following gives the average speed of the cat, in feet per second, over the first t seconds after the cat begins chasing the mouse, where $0 \le t \le 10$.

A) $9t^2$
B) $\frac{9t}{\sqrt{t}}$
C) $9t\sqrt{t}$
D) $3t\sqrt{t}$

10. The formula $E = \frac{1}{2}mv^2$ gives the kinetic energy E, in joules, of an object with mass m, in kilograms, that is moving with velocity v, in meters per second. A scientist uses the formula to find the kinetic energy of an object moving with velocity w and the kinetic energy of the same object moving with velocity $3.5w$. What is the ratio of the kinetic energy of the faster object to the kinetic energy of the slower object?

LESSON 4 – GEOMETRY
LINES AND ANGLES

LEVEL 1

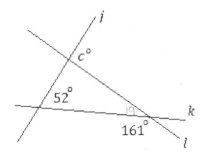

1. Intersecting lines j, k, and l are shown above. What is the value of c ?

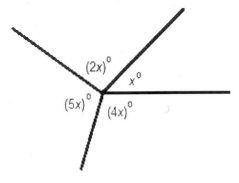

3. In the figure above, four line segments meet at a point to form four angles. What is the value of x?

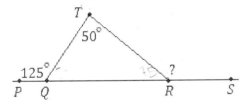

2. In the figure above, vertices Q and R of $\triangle QTR$ lie on $\overline{PS}$, the measure of $\angle PQT$ is 125°, and the measure of $\angle QTR$ is 50°. What is the measure of $\angle TRS$? (Disregard the degree symbol when gridding your answer.)

LEVEL 2

4. C is the midpoint of line segment $\overline{AB}$, and D and E are the midpoints of $\overline{AC}$ and $\overline{CB}$, respectively. If the length of $\overline{AB}$ is 17, what is the length of $\overline{DE}$?

A) 4.25
B) 6.75
C) 8.5
D) 17

13

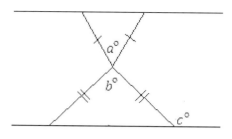

Note: Figure not drawn to scale.

5. In the figure above, the two triangles are isosceles. If $a + c = 175$ and $a = 22$, what is the value of b ?

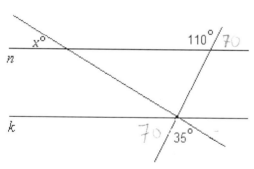

Note: Figure not drawn to scale.

6. In the figure above, what is the value of x?

LEVEL 3

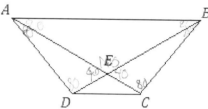

Note: Figure not drawn to scale.

7. On $\overline{AB}$ above, $CD = DB$. What is the length of $\overline{AB}$?

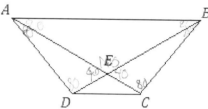

Note: Figure not drawn to scale.

8. In the figure above, $\overline{AC}$ and $\overline{BD}$ intersect at E, $AE = BE$, $CE = DE$, $m\angle AED = 40°$, and $m\angle BCE = 80°$. What is the measure, in degrees, of $\angle ABC$? (Disregard the degree symbol when gridding your answer.)

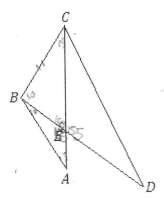

Note: Figure not drawn to scale.

9. In the figure above, $AB = BC$, $m\angle BCA = 15°$, $m\angle ABD = 10°$, and AC bisects $\angle BCD$. What is $m\angle CED$? (Disregard the degree symbol when gridding your answer.)

LEVEL 5

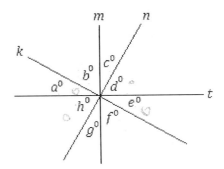

Note: Figure not drawn to scale.

10. In the figure above, lines k, m, n, and t intersect at a point. If $a + b + c = f + g + h$, which of the following must be true?

    I. $d = e$
    II. $a + b = f + h$
    III. $b + c = g + h$

A) I and II only
B) I and III only
C) II and III only
D) I, II, and III

15

LESSON 5 – HEART OF ALGEBRA
SOLVING LINEAR INEQUALITIES

LEVEL 1

1. What is the greatest integer x that satisfies the inequality $3 + \frac{x}{6} < 8$?

2. If $7t + 11 < 46$, which of the following CANNOT be the value of t ?

   A) 0
   B) 1
   C) 3
   D) 5

LEVEL 2

3. Which of the following ordered pairs (x, y) does not satisfy the inequality $7x - 2y < 3$?

   A) $(1, 4)$
   B) $(2, 10)$
   C) $(3, 11)$
   D) $(4, 12)$

LEVEL 3

4. Which of the following numbers is NOT a solution of the inequality $8x - 4 \geq 9x - 2$?

   A) -4
   B) -3
   C) -2
   D) -1

5. * A copacker has a maximum daily budget of $8000. The copacker makes n identical items, each costing $8 to produce. If the daily fixed costs to run the copacker's warehouse are $2300, what is the maximum possible value for n that will keep the combined daily fixed costs and production costs within the copacker's daily budget?

6. When 7 is increased by $5x$, the result is less than 62. What is the greatest possible integer value for x ?

7. Kayleigh plans to go skiing for the day. The ski rental costs $15 per hour, and the lift ticket is $50 for the day. Kaleigh wants to spend less than $130 for the lift ticket and the ski rental. If skis can be rented for only a whole number of hours, what is the maximum number of hours for which Kayleigh can ski?

LEVEL 4

8. * Jim makes watches that he sells at his store "Jim's watches." Jim pays $2980 each month in rent to keep his store. Each watch costs Jim $10 to make, and he sells each watch for $90. What is the least number of watches Jim needs to sell each month to cover the cost of his rent?

$$C = 15h + p + 2000$$

9. The formula above gives the weekly cost C, in dollars, of running a local pizza parlor, where h is the total number of hours the store is open and p is the number of pizzas made. If, during a particular week, the pizza parlor was open for at least 40 hours and it cost no more than $2,750 to run the pizza parlor, what is the maximum number of pizzas that could have been made?

LEVEL 5

10. * A worker earns $12 per hour for the first 40 hours he works in any given week, and $18 per hour for each hour above 40 that he works each week. If the worker saves 75% of his earnings each week, what is the least number of hours he must work in a week to save at least $441 for the week?

A) 6
B) 8
C) 46
D) 47

17

LESSON 6 – PASSPORT TO ADVANCED MATH
FUNCTIONS

LEVEL 1

1. For the function $f(x) = 7x^2 - 2x$, what is the value of $f(-5)$?

   A) -175
   B) -165
   C) 165
   D) 185

2. If $g(x) = \frac{x^3 - 2x + 5}{x^2 - 2}$, what is $g(-2)$?

   A) $-\frac{3}{2}$
   B) $-\frac{1}{6}$
   C) $\frac{1}{2}$
   D) $\frac{9}{2}$

3. If $f(x) = 3(x - 1) + 5$, which of the following is equivalent to $f(x)$?

   A) $8 - 3x$
   B) $3x - 8$
   C) $3x + 2$
   D) $3x + 4$

LEVEL 2

$$h(x) = kx^2 - 11$$

4. For the function h defined above, k is a constant and $h(3) = 19$. What is the value of $h(-3)$?

   A) -19
   B) 0
   C) 9
   D) 19

LEVEL 3

5. If $g(x - 5) = 2x + 7$ for all values of x, what is the value of $g(-1)$?

6. A function f satisfies $f(-6) = 1$ and $f(3) = 11$. A function g satisfies $g(-6) = 3$ and $g(1) = 5$. Find the value of $f(g(-6))$.

7. If $f(x) = -7x + 2$, which of the following is equivalent to $f(x + h)$?

    A) $-7x + h + 2$
    B) $-7(x + 7h) + 2$
    C) $-7x - 7h + 2$
    D) $-7x - 5h$

x	$f(x)$	$g(x)$
-1	2	2
3	6	2
5	5	5
8	-2	4

8. The table above shows some values of the functions f and g. For which of the following values of x is $f(x) + g(x) = f(x)g(x)$?

    A) -1
    B) 3
    C) 5
    D) 8

9. If $g(x) = -x^2 + 6x - 4$ and n is an integer greater than 4, what is one possible value of $g(n)$ for which $g(n)$ is positive?

LEVEL 4

$$f(x) = x^2 + 5x - 19$$
$$g(x) = 3 - f(x)$$
$$h(x) = \sqrt{g(x)}$$

10. For the functions f, g, and h defined above, what is the value of $h(1)$?

    A) -13
    B) 0
    C) 4
    D) 16

LESSON 7 – PROBLEM SOLVING
TABLES

LEVEL 1

Questions 1 - 4 refer to the following information.

	Microchip	No Microchip	Total
Cats	3	1	4
Dogs	4	3	7
Rabbits	1	4	5
Total	8	8	16

The table above shows the number of animals with and without microchips at an animal shelter.

1. How many of the dogs at the shelter do not have microchips?

2. Of the 16 animals at the shelter, how many are not cats?

3. What is the ratio of the number of dogs in the shelter to the number of animals in the shelter without microchips?

LEVEL 2

4. What fraction of the rabbits at the shelter do not have microchips?

   A) $\frac{1}{4}$

   B) $\frac{5}{16}$

   C) $\frac{1}{2}$

   D) $\frac{4}{5}$

Where Did People Hear About Company?	
Source	Percent who responded to survey
Friend or Family	51%
Email	15%
Direct Mailing	5%
Search Engine	18%
Other Source	11%

5. * A company sent out a survey to their clients to try to determine where their clients were hearing about them. The table above shows a summary of the 1800 responses they received. Based on the table, how many of those that responded to the survey found out about the company from a friend, a family member, or a search engine?

    A) 324
    B) 558
    C) 918
    D) 1242

LEVEL 3

		Entree	
		Chicken	Fish
Dessert	Ice Cream	34	27
	Cake	20	21

6. The table above shows the entrees and desserts chosen by 102 attendees of a wedding reception. Each attendee chose exactly one entrée and one dessert. Of the attendees who chose fish, what fraction chose ice cream as a desert?

    A) $\frac{27}{102}$

    B) $\frac{19}{46}$

    C) $\frac{23}{50}$

    D) $\frac{27}{48}$

Number of minutes Aki plans to run per day	120
Aki's average heartbeat, in beats per minute, while running	143
Number of steps Aki runs per minute	180
Total number of laps Aki plans to run during training	560
Total number of steps Aki plans to take during training	151,200

7. * Aki is planning to train for a marathon. The table above shows information about Aki's training. If Aki runs at the rates given in the table, which of the following is closest to the number of days it would take Aki to complete his training?

   A) 7
   B) 25
   C) 53
   D) 126

LEVEL 4

8. A square lawn measures 8 yards by 8 yards. Eight landscapers each mark off a randomly selected square region with side length 1 yard. There is no overlap between any of the regions. Each landscaper counts the number of weeds in the soil to a depth of 6 inches beneath the surface in each region. The results are shown in the table below.

Region	Number of weeds	Region	Number of weeds
I	30	V	31
II	25	VI	16
III	27	VII	36
IV	22	VIII	18

   Which of the following is a reasonable approximation of the number of weeds to a depth of 6 inches beneath the surface on the entire lawn?

   A)   25
   B)   200
   C)   1,600
   D) 12,800

22

Questions 9 - 10 refer to the following information.

Janet's Sunday Run		
Part of run	Distance (miles)	Average running speed (miles per hour)
From home to park entrance	0.2	8
Each lap around the park	0.5	12
From park entrance to home	1.4	6

Every Sunday, Janet goes for a run. She runs from her home to the park, followed by 3 laps around the park, and then she runs home. The table above shows the distance, in miles, and her typical average running speed, in miles per hour, for each part of her run.

9. One Sunday, Janet completed her entire run in exactly 30 minutes. What was her average speed, in miles per hour, during her run that Sunday?

10. * During one Sunday run, Janet decided to speed up for one of her 3 laps around the park, decreasing her total running time by 10%. Based on the table, how many fewer <u>minutes</u> does Janet take to finish her run than if she ran with her usual average running speed the whole way?

LESSON 8 – GEOMETRY
TRIANGLES

LEVEL 1

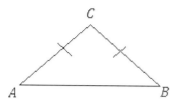

1. In $\triangle ABC$, the measure of $\angle B$ is 40°, and $\overline{AC} \cong \overline{BC}$, as shown in the figure above. What is the measure, in degrees, of $\angle C$? (Disregard the degree symbol when gridding your answer.)

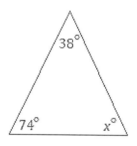

2. In the triangle above, what is the value of x ?

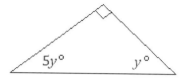

3. In the right triangle above, what is the value of y ?

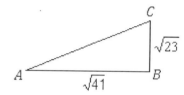

Note: Figure not drawn to scale.

4. In right triangle ABC above, what is the length of side AC ?

LEVEL 2

5. A basketball player runs due west x feet to receive a pass. He catches the basketball and then moves due north 24 feet. If the basketball player winds up 26 feet from his starting point, what is the value of x ?

LEVEL 3

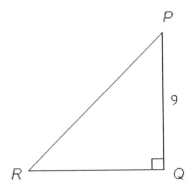

6. In the isosceles right triangle above, $PQ = 9$. What is the length, in inches, of $\overline{PR}$?

A) $9\sqrt{2}$
B) $\sqrt{18}$
C) 18
D) 9

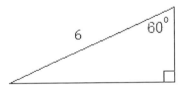

7. The figure above shows a right triangle whose hypotenuse is 6 feet long. How many feet long is the longer leg of this triangle?

A) 3
B) 12
C) $\sqrt{3}$
D) $3\sqrt{3}$

LEVEL 4

8. If x is an integer, how many different triangles are there with sides of length 1, 2, and x ?

A) None
B) One
C) Two
D) Three

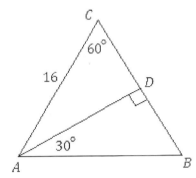

9. In $\triangle ABC$ above, what is the length of $\overline{BD}$?

A) 4
B) 8
C) $8\sqrt{2}$
D) $8\sqrt{3}$

LEVEL 5

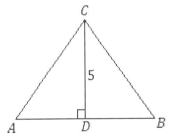

10. $\triangle ABC$ shown above is equilateral, $\overline{CD}$ is an altitude, and $CD = 5$. What is the length of a side of $\triangle ABC$?

A) $\frac{5\sqrt{3}}{3}$
B) $\frac{10\sqrt{3}}{3}$
C) $5\sqrt{3}$
D) $10\sqrt{3}$

LESSON 9 – HEART OF ALGEBRA
SETTING UP LINEAR EXPRESSIONS

LEVEL 1

1. An SAT course is available as a book and as an app. The author of the course earns $5.72 for each book sale and $2.85 for each app download. Which of the following expressions represents the amount, in dollars, that the author of the course earns if b books are sold and a apps are downloaded?

   A) $5.72b + 2.85a$
   B) $5.72b - 2.85a$
   C) $2.85b + 5.72a$
   D) $2.85b - 5.72a$

2. Last Sunday, Samuel ran c errands per hour for 2 hours and Timothy ran d errands per hour for 4 hours. Which of the following represents the total number of errands run by Samuel and Timothy last Sunday?

   A) $2c + 4d$
   B) $2d + 4c$
   C) $6cd$
   D) $8cd$

3. A juggler is hired to perform for 35 children at a birthday party. He will be paid $50 per hour and an additional $75 tip if he stays for the whole party. If the juggler stays for the whole party, which of the following expressions can be used to determine how much the juggler earns, in dollars?

   A) $75x + (50 + 35)$, where x is the number of children
   B) $(50 + 35)x + 75$, where x is the number of children
   C) $75x + 50$, where x is the number of hours
   D) $50x + 75$, where x is the number of hours

4. To stay healthy, it is recommended that one walks 10,000 steps per day. Hootan currently walks 5000 steps per day. He plans to increase his number of steps per day by 220 steps each week. Which of the following represents the number of steps per day that Hootan will be taking w weeks from now?

   A) $220 + 5000w$
   B) $5000 + 220w$
   C) $5000 - 220w$
   D) $10,000 + 220w$

LEVEL 2

5. A carpenter is building cabinets for a homeowner. The carpenter charges c dollars per hour plus a flat fee of m dollars for lumber. If the carpenter charges $750 for a 3-hour job, which of the following represents the relationship between c and m ?

    A) $750 = c - 3m$
    B) $750 = 3m - c$
    C) $750 = 3c + m$
    D) $750 = c + 3m$

6. The number of veterinarians working in an animal hospital between 1970 and 1985 was three times the number of veterinarians working in the same animal hospital between 1985 and 2000. If there were 18 veterinarians working in the animal hospital between 1970 and 1985 and there were n veterinarians working in the animal hospital between 1985 and 2000, which of the following equations is true?

    A) $n + 18 = 3$
    B) $\frac{n}{3} = 18$
    C) $3n = 18$
    D) $18n = 3$

LEVEL 3

7. In 2012, Timothy had a collection consisting of 123 comic books. Starting in 2013, Timothy has been collecting 15 comic books per year. At this rate, if t is the number of years after 2012, which of the following functions C gives the number of comic books Timothy will have?

    A) $C(t) = 15 + 123t$
    B) $C(t) = 123 + 15t$
    C) $C(t) = 2012 + 123t$
    D) $C(t) = 2012 + 15t$

8. Tammy and Yeeshing went out to lunch. The price of Tammy's meal was m dollars, and the price of Yeeshing's meal was $5 more than the price of Tammy's meal. If Tammy and Yeeshing split the cost of the meals evenly and each paid a 22% tip, which of the following expressions represents the amount, in dollars, each of them paid? (Assume there is no sales tax.)

    A) $2.44m + 6.10$
    B) $1.22m + 6.10$
    C) $1.22m + 3.05$
    D) $0.22m + 0.5$

27

LEVEL 5

9. A scientist studying mouse behavior created a maze with an entrance consisting of three different paths. Two of the paths required traveling up an incline, whereas the third path was flat. The scientist wished to test the tendency for a mouse to choose the flat path over the inclined paths. Over the course of a day, 100 mice were placed at the entrance to the maze. Of the first 50 mice, 21 chose to move along the flat path. Among the remaining 50 mice, n mice chose to move along the flat path. Assuming that more than 35% of the 100 mice chose to move along the flat path, which of the following inequalities best describes the possible values of n ?

A) $n + 21 > 0.35 \cdot 100$, where $n \le 50$
B) $n - 21 > 0.35 \cdot 100$, where $n \le 50$
C) $n > 0.35(100 - 21)$, where $n \le 50$
D) $n > 0.35(100 + 21)$, where $n \le 50$

10. A publisher spends an average of $12,500 per year in distribution fees. The distributer is offering the option of a one-time fee of $40,000 in exchange for reducing distribution costs to a fixed fee of $3700 per year. Which of the following inequalities can be solved to find t, the number of years after which the savings on distribution costs will exceed the one-time distribution fee?

A) $40,000 > \frac{12,500}{3700}t$
B) $40,000 - 12,500 > 3700t$
C) $40,000 > (12,500 - 3700)t$
D) $40,000 < (12,500 - 3700)t$

28

LESSON 10 – PASSPORT TO ADVANCED MATH
GRAPHS OF FUNCTIONS

LEVEL 1

Questions 1 - 6 refer to the following information.

The entire graph of the function g is shown in the xy-plane below.

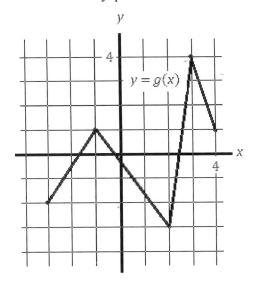

LEVEL 2

1.   What is the value of $g(4) - g(-3)$?

   A) -1
   B) 1
   C) 2
   D) 3

LEVEL 3

2.   For what value of x is the value of $g(x)$ at its maximum?

   A) -1
   B) 2
   C) 3
   D) 4

3. What is the maximum value of g ?

    A) -1
    B) 1
    C) 3
    D) 4

4. For how many values of x between -3 and 4 does $g(x) = -2.5$?

    A) None
    B) One
    C) Two
    D) More than two

5. If the function h is defined by $h(x) = -g(x)$, which of the following points is on the graph of h ?

    A) $(3, 4)$
    B) $(3, -4)$
    C) $(-3, 4)$
    D) $(-3, -4)$

6. Which of the following expressions does NOT represent the positive difference between the maximum and minimum values of g on the interval $-3 \le x \le 4$?

    A) $g(3) - g(2)$
    B) $g(3 - 2)$
    C) $|g(2) - g(3)|$
    D) $4 - (-3)$

7. In the xy-plane, the point $(-3, 7)$ lies on the graph of the function $h(x) = 5x^2 - kx + 1$. What is the value of $|k|$?

8. The range of the polynomial function p is the set of real numbers greater than or equal to -3, and the zeros of p are -2 and 3. Which of the following could be the graph of $y = p(x)$ in the xy-plane?

A)

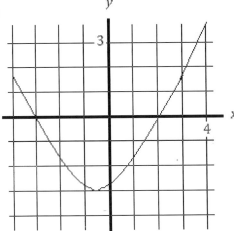

B)

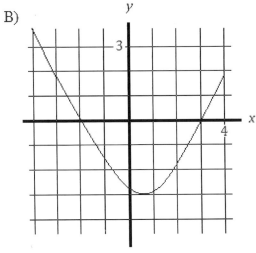

C)

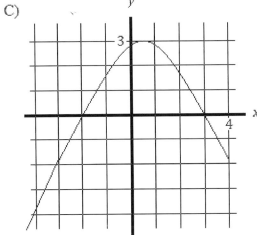

D)

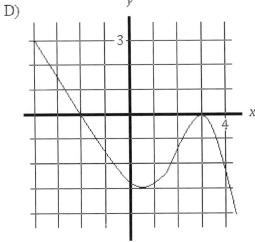

LEVEL 4

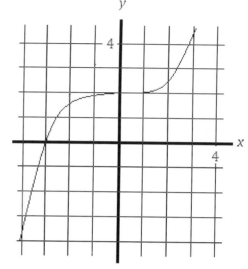

x	$f(x)$
-3	0
-2	2
-1	3
0	1
1	4

9. Selected values for the function f are shown in the table above, and the graph of the function g is shown in the xy-plane above. For which of the following values of x is $f(x) < g(x)$?

A) -3
B) -2
C) -1
D) 0

LEVEL 5

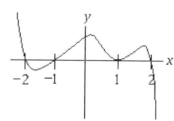

10. Which of the following could be an equation for the graph shown in the xy-plane above?

A) $y = (x - 2)(x - 1)(x + 1)(x + 2)$
B) $y = (x - 2)(x - 1)^2(x + 1)(x + 2)$
C) $y = (2 - x)(x - 1)^2(x + 1)(x + 2)$
D) $y = (2 - x)(x - 1)^3(x + 1)(x + 2)$

LESSON 11 – PROBLEM SOLVING GRAPHS

LEVEL 1

Questions 1 - 5 refer to the following information.

A honeybee scout leaves his swarm for 2 and a half hours to search for a new home. The graph below shows the honeybee's distance from his swarm over the 2-hour period for which he was gone. The honeybee stopped to rest on a leaf for 20 minutes during his search.

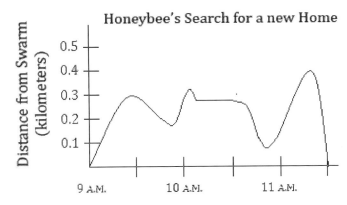

1. Based on the graph, which of the following is closest to the time the honeybee landed on the leaf and began resting?

   A) 9:30 A.M.
   B) 9:45 A.M.
   C) 10:10 A.M.
   D) 10:40 A.M.

2. During which of the following time periods was the distance between the honeybee and his swarm strictly decreasing?

   A) Between 9:30 A.M. and 10:00 A.M.
   B) Between 10:00 A.M. and 10:10 A.M.
   C) Between 10:30 A.M. and 10:45 A.M.
   D) Between 11:00 A.M. and 11:30 A.M.

3. During which of the following time periods was the distance between the honeybee and his swarm strictly decreasing, then strictly increasing?

    A) Between 9:30 A.M. and 10:00 A.M.
    B) Between 10:00 A.M. and 10:10 A.M.
    C) Between 10:30 A.M. and 10:45 A.M.
    D) Between 11:00 A.M. and 11:30 A.M.

4. Based on the graph, which of the following is closest to the time the honeybee is farthest from his swarm?

    A) 10:05 A.M.
    B) 10:50 A.M.
    C) 11:20 A.M.
    D) 11:30 A.M.

5. Based on the graph, which statement is true?

    A) The honeybee's maximum distance from the swarm is reached about 1 hour and 15 minutes after he leaves the swarm.
    B) The honeybee's distance from the swarm steadily increases for the first hour after he leaves the swarm.
    C) The honeybee's minimum distance from the swarm during the second hour is approximately 1 kilometer.
    D) The honeybee's minimum distance from the swarm during the second half hour is greater than the honeybee's minimum distance from the swarm during the fourth half hour.

LEVEL 2

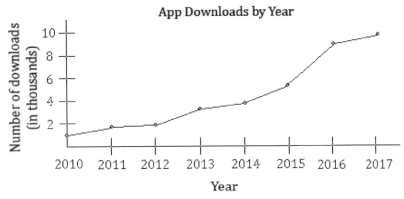

App Downloads by Year

6. A small company released an app in early 2010. The number of downloads each year is shown in the line graph above. According to the graph, between which two consecutive years was there the greatest change in the number of app downloads?

A) 2010 − 2011
B) 2014 − 2015
C) 2015 − 2016
D) 2016 − 2017

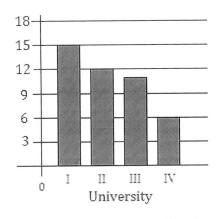

7. The number of students attending 4 universities is shown in the graph above. If the total number of students is 4350, what is an appropriate label for the vertical axis of the graph?

A) Number of students (in tens)
B) Number of students (in hundreds)
C) Number of students (in thousands)
D) Number of students (in tens of thousands)

LEVEL 3

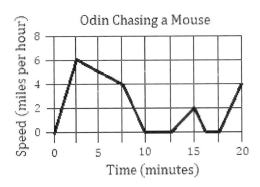

8. Odin the cat chased a mouse for twenty minutes. His time and speed are displayed in the graph above. According to the graph, which of the following statements concerning Odin's chase is true?

A) Odin's speed decreased at a constant rate for 10 minutes sometime during the chase.
B) Odin's speed reached its maximum during the last five minutes of the chase.
C) Odin never stopped during the chase.
D) While Odin was moving, his speed was never constant.

Questions 9 and 10 refer to the following information.

A bird species called a *garret* is best known for "plunge diving" to catch fish. The graph below shows the height of a garret over a period of 1 minute as it dives for fish.

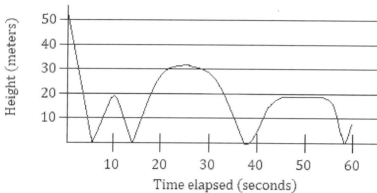

9. During the 1 minute period, how many times was the garret at a height of 25 meters?

   A) One
   B) Two
   C) Three
   D) More than three

10. Of the following, which best approximates the maximum height, in meters, of the garret between the second and third time it hit the water?

    A) 50
    B) 32
    C) 25
    D) 19

LESSON 12 – GEOMETRY
CIRCLES

LEVEL 1

1. An angle with a measure of 45° has a measure of x radians, where $0 \leq x < 2\pi$. What is the value of x ?

   A) $\frac{1}{4}$

   B) $\frac{1}{2}$

   C) $\frac{\pi}{4}$

   D) $\frac{\pi}{2}$

2. What is the diameter of a circle whose area is 36π ?

   A) 6

   B) 12

   C) 36

   D) 12π

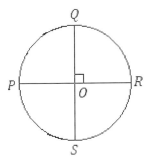

3. In the circle above with center O, the length of minor arc $\overparen{PQ}$ is 5. What is the circumference of the circle?

   A) 10

   B) 20

   C) 25

   D) 30

LEVEL 2

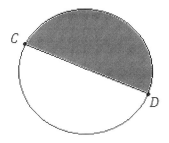

4. In the circle above, segment CD is a diameter. If the area of the shaded region is 32π, what is the length of the diameter of the circle?

   A) 4

   B) 8

   C) 12

   D) 16

LEVEL 3

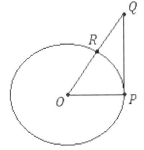

Note: Figure not drawn to scale.

5. In the figure above, the circle has center O and line segment $\overline{PQ}$ is tangent to the circle at point P. If $PQ = 1.2$ and the length of a diameter of the circle is 1, what is the length of $\overline{RQ}$?

LEVEL 4

6. Points P and Q lie on a circle with diameter 4, and arc $\widehat{PQ}$ has length $\frac{\pi}{4}$. What fraction of the circumference of the circle is the length of arc $\widehat{PQ}$?

7. In a circle with center O, central angle POQ has a measure of $\frac{\pi}{3}$ radians. The area of the sector formed by central angle POQ is what fraction of the area of the circle?

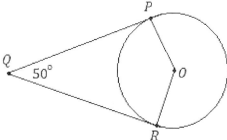

8. In the figure above, O is the center of the circle, line segments PQ and RQ are tangent to the circle at points P and R, respectively. The two segments intersect at point Q as shown. If the length of minor arc $\widehat{PR}$ is 13, what is the circumference of the circle?

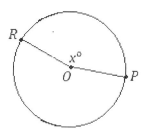

Note: Figure not drawn to scale.

9. * In the figure above, O is the center of the circle, and the radius of the circle is 6. If the length of arc $\widehat{PR}$ is between 16 and 17, what is one possible integer value of x ?

LEVEL 5

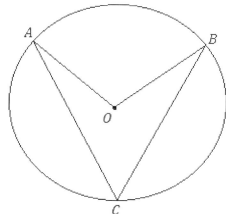

Note: Figure not drawn to scale.

10. In the circle above with center O, $m\angle CAO = m\angle CBO = 30°$. What is $m\angle AOB$? (Disregard the degree symbol when gridding your answer.)

 **LESSON 13 – HEART OF ALGEBRA**
ADDITIONAL PRACTICE 1

LEVEL 1

1. If $5k = 7$, what is the value of $10k + 2$?

   A) $\frac{7}{5}$
   B) 10
   C) 14
   D) 16

2. If $3k - 5 \geq 7$, which of the following CANNOT be the value of k ?

   A) 3
   B) 4
   C) 5
   D) 6

3. A hose is used to fill a swimming pool with water. When the hose is turned on, the pool fills up with water at the rate of 10 gallons per minute. If the pool initially contains 200 gallons of water, which of the following equations can be used to express the amount of water A in the pool, in gallons, t minutes after the hose is turned on?

   A) $A = 10t$
   B) $A = 10t + 200$
   C) $A = 10t - 200$
   D) $A = 200t + 10$

LEVEL 2

4. Which of the following ordered pairs (x, y) satisfies the inequality $2x - 5y \geq -5$?

   A) $(1, 2)$
   B) $(2, 3)$
   C) $(3, 3)$
   D) $(3, 2)$

5. If $\frac{13}{5}x - \frac{6}{5}x = \frac{7}{2} + \frac{7}{6}$, what is the value of x ?

7. A private club is accepting k new members each month. Assuming that there were m members in the club at the beginning of this month, which function best models the total number of members, T, the club plans to have n months from now?

    A) $T = kn + m$
    B) $T = kn - m$
    C) $T = m(k)^n$
    D) $T = k(m)^n$

LEVEL 3

6. Jamie currently has 350 "friends" on a popular social media site. Her goal is to have at least 800 "friends" within the next 15 weeks. What is the minimum number of "friends" per week, on average, she needs to make?

    A) 22
    B) 25
    C) 28
    D) 30

8. What value of x is the solution of the equation $3.4(x - 1) = 2x + 1.6$?

LEVEL 4

9. Brandon needs to get his car repaired. Barry's Auto Repair gives Brandon an estimate of $300 in parts and $5 per minute in labor costs. Sentinel Mechanics gives Brandon an estimate of $200 in parts and $7 per minute in labor costs. Let t represent the number of minutes that it takes to complete the repairs, and assume that the two repair shops will take the same amount of time. What are all values of t for which Barry's Auto Repair's total charge is less than Sentinel Mechanics' total charge?

   A) $t < 20$
   B) $20 \le t \le 35$
   C) $35 \le t \le 50$
   D) $t > 50$

10. Tanglewood Lumber's revenue decreased from $22 million in 1990 to $17.5 million in 2007. If Tanglewood Lumber's revenue decreased at a constant rate, which of the following linear functions R best models the revenue, in millions of dollars, t years after 1990 ?

   A) $R(t) = \frac{9}{34}t + 22$
   B) $R(t) = -\frac{9}{34}t + 22$
   C) $R(t) = \frac{35}{34}t + 22$
   D) $R(t) = -\frac{35}{34}t + 22$

11. For 7 consecutive even integers, the sum of the first, fourth, and fifth integer is 40 less than 5 times the sixth integer. What is the seventh integer?

LEVEL 5

12. An ornithologist oversees a 400-acre bird sanctuary with only two types of birds: egrets and flamingos. There are currently 150 egrets and 200 flamingos living within the sanctuary. If 75 more egrets are introduced into the sanctuary, how many more flamingos must be introduced so that $\frac{5}{6}$ of the total number of birds in the sanctuary are flamingos?

41

LESSON 14 – PASSPORT TO ADVANCED MATH
ADDITIONAL PRACTICE 1

LEVEL 1

$$g(x) = \frac{2x - 5}{3}$$

1. For the function g above, what is the value of $g(-11)$?

   A) -9
   B) -6
   C) -3
   D) $-\frac{5}{3}$

2. If $14xz - 21yz = az(2x - by)$, where a and b are positive real numbers, what is the value of $a + b$?

LEVEL 2

$$f(x) = \frac{2}{5}x + k$$

3. In the function above, k is a constant. If $f(10) = 3$, what is the value of $f(-15)$?

   A) -7
   B) -1
   C) 5
   D) 7

4. Which of the following functions has a graph in the xy-plane for which y is always greater than -5 ?

   A) $f(x) = x^3 - 4$
   B) $f(x) = x^2 - 5$
   C) $f(x) = (x - 2)^2 - 5$
   D) $f(x) = |x - 3| - 4$

LEVEL 3

5. Which of the following is equivalent to the expression $(x - 5)^2 - 9$?

A) $x^2 + 16$
B) $x^2 - 10x - 9$
C) $(x - 2)(x - 8)$
D) $(x - 2)(x + 8)$

6. If $f(x) = -5x - 2$, what is $f(-3x)$ equal to?

A) $15x^2 + 6x$
B) $15x + 2$
C) $15x - 2$
D) $-15x + 2$

7. In the xy-plane, the point $(3, 1)$ lies on the graph of the function g. If $g(x) = a - 2x^2$, where a is a constant, what is the value of a ?

LEVEL 4

$$g(x) = \frac{3x + 6}{5x^2 - 20x + 15}$$

8. For the rational function defined above, which of the following is an equivalent form that displays values that are not included in the domain of the function as constants or coefficients?

A) $g(x) = \frac{3}{5x^2}$

B) $g(x) = \frac{3}{5x - 15}$

C) $g(x) = \frac{3(x+2)}{5(x^2 - 4x + 3)}$

D) $g(x) = \frac{3(x+2)}{5(x-1)(x-3)}$

43

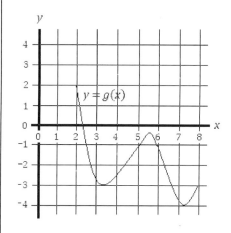

x	$h(x)$
-4	3
-3	1
-2	5
-1	2
0	0
1	7
2	6

9. The graph of the function g and a table of values for the function h are shown above. The minimum value of g is a. What is the value of $h(a)$?

LEVEL 5

$$y = ax^2 - b$$

10. In the equation above, a and b are positive constants. Which of the following is an equivalent form of the equation?

   A) $y = (ax - b)(ax + b)$
   B) $y = (ax - \sqrt{b})(ax + \sqrt{b})$
   C) $y = (\sqrt{a}x - \sqrt{b})(\sqrt{a}x + \sqrt{b})$
   D) $y = (ax + b)^2$

11. For which of the following functions is it true that $f(-x) = -f(x)$ for all values of x ?

   A) $f(x) = x^2 + 5$
   B) $f(x) = x^2 + 5x$
   C) $f(x) = x^3 + 5x$
   D) $f(x) = x^3 + 5$

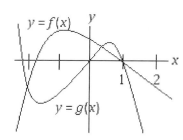

12. Graphs of the functions f and g are shown in the xy-plane above. For which of the following values of x does $g(x) = -f(x)$?

   A) $\frac{1}{2}$
   B) 0
   C) -1
   D) -2

LESSON 15 – PROBLEM SOLVING
ADDITIONAL PRACTICE 1

LEVEL 1

1. Johanna began filling a pitcher with water and then stopped for a short while. She then began filling the pitcher with water again, but at a slower rate than she had initially. Which of the following graphs could model the total amount of water in the pitcher versus time?

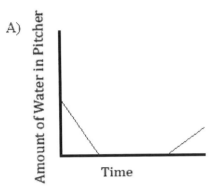

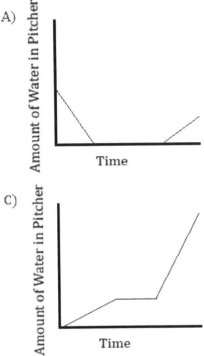

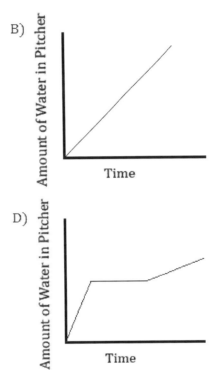

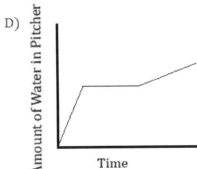

2. There are 4 atoms of carbon and 10 atoms of hydrogen in one molecule of butane. How many atoms of carbon are there in 17 molecules of butane?

LEVEL 2

3. * A *ream* of paper consists of 500 sheets stacked one on top of the other. Given that a ream of paper is 2 inches tall, which of the following is closest to the number of sheets of paper that need to be stacked to attain a height of $5\frac{3}{8}$ inches?

   A) 11
   B) 185
   C) 1340
   D) 5375

4. A store owner buys and sells watches, always keeping track of how many watches he has available for sale in his store. This data is shown on the graph below.

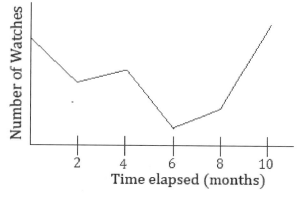

On what interval did the number of watches increase the fastest?

   A) Between 2 and 4 months
   B) Between 4 and 6 months
   C) Between 6 and 8 months
   D) Between 8 and 10 months

LEVEL 3

5. * After adding 5% sales tax, a hat costs $12.60. What is the price of the hat before adding the sales tax?

   A) $11.80
   B) $12.00
   C) $12.10
   D) $12.20

Questions 6 - 7 refer to the following information.

	2000	2001	2002	2003
Annual Donations for a Corporation, 2000-2003				
Animals	30	32	35	37.5
Children	380	410	425	438
Environment	36	37.5	38.25	40.1
Doctors	52	57	68	64
Scholarships	80	72	90.5	120.5

The table above lists the money donated annually by a corporation, in hundreds of dollars, to each of five causes from 2000 to 2003.

6. * Of the following, which ratio of the money donated to a cause in 2003 to the money donated to the same cause in 2000 is closest to the ratio of the money donated to animals in 2003 to the money donated to animals in 2000 ?

A) Children
B) Environment
C) Doctors
D) Scholarships

7. Find the average rate of change per year in the money donated to the environment from 2000 to 2003, to the nearest whole number of dollars.

LEVEL 4

Questions 8 - 11 refer to the following information.

A wheel with a diameter of 6 feet is rolling on the ground at a constant rate of 4 feet per second in a straight line from point a to point b.

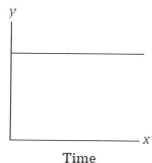

I

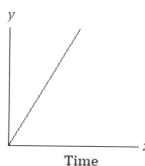

II

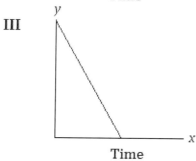

III

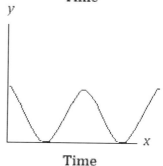

IV

8. Which of the graphs above could represent the distance of the center of the wheel from point a ?

    A) I
    B) II
    C) III
    D) IV

9. Which of the graphs above could represent the speed at which the wheel is rolling?

    A) I
    B) II
    C) III
    D) IV

10. Which of the graphs above could represent the distance from the center of the wheel to a fixed point on the rim?

    A) I
    B) II
    C) III
    D) IV

11. Which of the graphs above could represent the distance from the ground to a fixed point on the rim?

    A) I
    B) II
    C) III
    D) IV

48

LEVEL 5

12. Tom drives an average of 150 miles each day. His car can travel an average of 22 miles per gallon of gasoline. Tom would like to reduce his daily expenditure on gasoline by $6. Assuming gasoline costs $3 per gallon, which equation can Tom use to determine how many fewer average miles, d, he should drive each day?

A) $\frac{22}{3}d = 146$

B) $\frac{22}{3}d = 6$

C) $\frac{3}{22}d = 146$

D) $\frac{3}{22}d = 6$

LESSON 16 – GEOMETRY
ADDITIONAL PRACTICE 1

LEVEL 1

1. In isosceles triangle $\triangle PQR$, $\angle P$ and $\angle Q$ are congruent and the measure of $\angle R$ is 72°. What is the measure of $\angle P$? (Disregard the degree symbol when gridding your answer.)

    A) 18°
    B) 36°
    C) 54°
    D) 108°

2. What is the radius of a circle whose circumference is 15π ?

LEVEL 2

3. C is the midpoint of line segment $\overline{AB}$, and D and E are the midpoints of $\overline{AC}$ and $\overline{CB}$, respectively. If the length of $\overline{CB}$ is 3, what is the length of $\overline{DB}$?

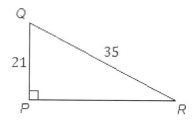

4. The lengths of two sides of right triangle $\triangle QPR$ shown above are given in centimeters. The midpoint of $\overline{PR}$ is how many centimeters from R ?

50

5. An angle with a measure of $\frac{5\pi}{3}$ radians has a measure of x degrees, where $0 \le x < 360$. What is the value of x ?

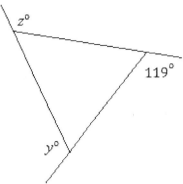

Note: Figure not drawn to scale.

7. In the figure above, what is the value of $y + z$?

LEVEL 3

6. In $\triangle ABC$, the length of $\overline{AB}$ is 7 centimeters, and the length of $\overline{BC}$ is 9 centimeters. If it can be determined, what is the length, in centimeters, of $\overline{AC}$?

   A) 2
   B) $4\sqrt{2}$
   C) $\sqrt{130}$
   D) It cannot be determined from the given information.

8. The number of radians in a 900-degree angle is equal to $k\pi$, where k is a positive constant. What is the value of k ?

LEVEL 4

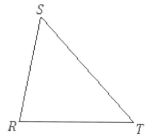

9.   In the triangle above, $RS = RT = 10$ and $ST = 12$. What is the area of the triangle?

10. In a circle with center O, central angle POQ has a measure of $\frac{5\pi}{6}$ radians. The area of the sector formed by central angle POQ is what fraction of the area of the circle?

LEVEL 5

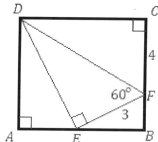

Note: Figure not drawn to scale.

11. $ABCD$ shown above is a square, $m\angle DFE = 60°$, $EF = 3$, and $CF = 4$. What is the area of square $ABCD$?

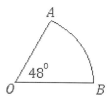

12. * In the figure above, AB is the arc of a circle with center O. If the length of arc AB is π, what is the area of region OAB, to the nearest tenth?

LESSON 17 – HEART OF ALGEBRA
EQUATIONS OF LINES AND THEIR GRAPHS

LEVEL 1

1. In the xy-plane, what is the y-intercept of the line with equation $y = -2x - 3$?

    A) $-\frac{1}{2}$

    B) -2

    C) $-\frac{3}{2}$

    D) -3

2. In the standard (x, y) coordinate plane, what is the slope of the line segment joining the points $(-3, -4)$ and $(5, -2)$?

LEVEL 2

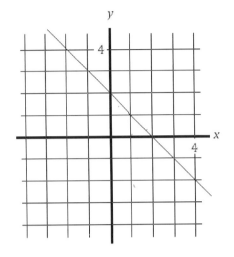

3. Which of the following is an equation of the line shown in the xy-plane above?

    A) $y = 2$
    B) $x = 2$
    C) $y = -x$
    D) $y = -x + 2$

4. What is the slope of the line with equation $y = \frac{x-5}{3}$?

LEVEL 3

5. The graph of the linear function h has intercepts at $(a, 0)$ and $(0, b)$ in the xy-plane. If a and b are opposite in sign, which of the following is true about te slope of the graph of h ?

   A) It is zero.
   B) It is positive.
   C) It is negative.
   D) It is undefined.

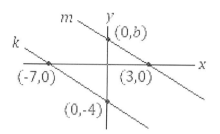

7. In the xy-plane above, line k is parallel to line m. What is the value of b ?

x	$g(x)$
0	-2
3	9
5	20

6. Some values of the linear function g are shown in the table above. Which of the following defines g ?

   A) $g(x) = \frac{10}{3}x - 2$

   B) $g(x) = \frac{11}{3}x - 2$

   C) $g(x) = 4x + 2$

   D) $g(x) = -2x$

LEVEL 4

$$-5x + 2y = 3$$

8. In the xy-plane, the graph of which of the following equations is perpendicular to the graph of the equation above?

   A) $5x + 2y = 1$
   B) $5x - 2y = 1$
   C) $2x + 5y = 1$
   D) $2x - 5y = 1$

9. The graph of a line in the (x, y)-plane passes through the points $(-1, 2)$ and $(3, -4)$. The graph of a second line has slope 1 and contains the point $(-2, 5)$. If the two lines intersect at the point (x, y), what is the value of $x + 3$?

LEVEL 5

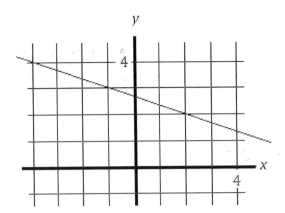

10. The graph of the linear function g is shown in the xy-plane above. The slope of the graph of the linear equation f is 5 times the slope of the graph of g. If the graph of f passes through the point $(0, 2)$, what is the value of $f(6)$?

A) -8
B) -4
C) 0
D) 12

LESSON 18 – PASSPORT TO ADVANCED MATH
OPERATIONS ON POLYNOMIALS

LEVEL 1

1. Which of the following is equivalent to the sum of $2x^2 - 3$ and $5x + 3$?

   A) $10x^3 + 3x$
   B) $10x^3$
   C) $7x^3$
   D) $2x^2 + 5x$

LEVEL 2

$$3x^2 + 5x - 2$$
$$4x^2 - 8x + 3$$

2. Which of the following is the sum of the two polynomials shown above?

   A) $7x^2 - 3x + 1$
   B) $7x^2 + 3x + 1$
   C) $7x^4 - 3x^2 + 1$
   D) $7x^4 + 3x^2 + 1$

$$(-3x^3 + 2x) - (-3x^3 - 2x)$$

3. Which of the following is equivalent to the expression above?

   A) 0
   B) $-6x^3$
   C) $4x$
   D) $-6x^3 + 4x$

4. When we subtract $-3x^2 + 2x - 5$ from $5x^2 + x - 3$, the result can be written $ax^2 + bx + c$, where a, b, and c are real numbers. What is the value of ac ?

LEVEL 3

$$(3217 + x + 1000x^2) + 200(30x^2 - x + 10)$$

5. The expression above can be written in the form $ax^2 + bx + c$, where a, b, and c are constants. What is the value of $a + b - c$?

LEVEL 4

6. * Which of the following is an equivalent form of $(3.5x^2 - 1.6) - (1.2x - 3.2)^2$?

   A) $2.06x^2 + 7.68x - 11.84$
   B) $2.06x^2 + 7.68x - 8.64$
   C) $4.94x^2 + 11.84$
   D) $4.94x^2 - 8.64$

LEVEL 5

7. Which of the following expressions is equivalent to $\left(\frac{x}{3}+\frac{y}{4}\right)^2$?

    A) $\frac{x^2}{3}+\frac{y^2}{4}$

    B) $\frac{x^2}{9}+\frac{y^2}{16}$

    C) $\frac{x^2}{9}+\frac{xy}{12}+\frac{y^2}{16}$

    D) $\frac{x^2}{9}+\frac{xy}{6}+\frac{y^2}{16}$

$$\frac{x^2-4x+3}{x-5}$$

8. Which of the following is equivalent to the expression above?

    A) $x+3-\frac{24}{x-5}$

    B) $x+3-\frac{12}{x-5}$

    C) $x+1+\frac{8}{x-5}$

    D) $x+1+\frac{3}{x-5}$

9. For a polynomial $p(x)$, the value of $p(2)$ is -5. Which of the following must be true about $p(x)$?

    A) $x-7$ is a factor of $p(x)$.
    B) $x-5$ is a factor of $p(x)$.
    C) $x+5$ is a factor of $p(x)$.
    D) The remainder when $p(x)$ is divided by $x-2$ is -5.

$$g(x) = x^2 + 4x - 1$$
$$h(x) = 2x^3 + 3x^2 + x$$

10. The polynomials g and h are defined above. Which of the following polynomials is divisible by $2x-1$?

    A) $k(x) = g(x) - h(x)$
    B) $k(x) = 12g(x) - h(x)$
    C) $k(x) = g(x) - 10h(x)$
    D) $k(x) = 12g(x) - 10h(x)$

LESSON 19 – PROBLEM SOLVING
STATISTICS

LEVEL 1

1. * The average (arithmetic mean) of four numbers is 73.6. If three of the numbers are 76.4, 92.3, and 85.2, what is the fourth number?

2. What is the median of the following 9 test grades?

$$89, 66, 75, 91, 56, 92, 76, 71, 76$$

3. What is the range of the median grades from the classes in the table above?

Exam Grade for Classes in a Middle School	
Class	Median grade (out of 100)
Algebra	65.5
Geometry	62
Chemistry	58.5
Physics	67
Spanish	75
History	82.5

LEVEL 2

Height of Student (in inches)

48	60	60	60	61	61	62
63	63	65	65	65	65	65
65	65	66	67	67	68	70
70	71	72	73	73	73	74

4. The table above lists the heights, to the nearest inch, of a random sample of 28 students. The outlier height of 48 inches is an error. Of the mean, median, mode, and range of the values listed, which will change the most if the 48-inch outlier is removed from the data?

A) Mean
B) Median
C) Mode
D) Range

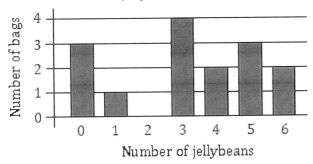

Number of Jellybeans in Each of 15 Bags

5. * Based on the histogram above, what is the average (arithmetic mean) number of jellybeans per bag?

Time on Treadmill (minutes)	Frequency
15	1
20	3
25	2
30	1
35	2
40	3
45	3
50	1
55	1
60	1

7. A personal trainer with 18 clients recorded how much time each client spent on the treadmill at their last session. The results are shown in the table above. Based on the table, what was the median number of minutes that the trainer's clients spent on the treadmill?

LEVEL 3

6. Vlada is preparing for the SAT. Her goal is to study an average of at least 6 hours per week for 5 weeks. She studied 4 hours the first week, 7 hours the second week, 8 hours the third week, and 3 hours the fourth week. Which inequality can be used to represent the number of hours, h, Vlada could study on the fifth week to reach her goal?

A) $\frac{4+7+8+3}{4} + h \geq 6$

B) $4 + 7 + 8 + 3 \geq h \cdot 6$

C) $\frac{4}{5} + \frac{7}{5} + \frac{8}{5} + \frac{3}{5} + h \geq 6$

D) $4 + 7 + 8 + 3 + h \geq 5 \cdot 6$

LEVEL 4

	Heights (inches)							
Jessie	5.3	4.1	4.7	6.2	3.8	4.5	4.8	5.9
Carl	3.8	2.7	4.9	6.1	x	5.1	2.9	3.9

8. * Jessie and Carl each collected eight plants, and the heights of the plants are given in the table above. The mean of the heights of the plants collected by Jessie is 0.3 inches more than the mean of the heights of the plants collected by Carl. What is the value of x ?

LEVEL 5

9. If x is the average (arithmetic mean) of a and b, y is the average of $2a$ and $3b$, and z is the average of $4a$ and $5b$, what is the average of x, y, and z in terms of a and b ?

    A) $a + b$
    B) $\frac{a+b}{2}$
    C) $\frac{7a}{3} + 3b$
    D) $\frac{7a+9b}{6}$

10. In Dr. Steve's AP Calculus BC class, students are given a grade between 0 and 100, inclusive on each exam. Jason's average (arithmetic mean) for the first 3 exams was 90. What is the lowest grade Jason can receive on his 4th exam and still be able to have an average of 90 for all 7 exams that will be given?

LESSON 20 – GEOMETRY
SOLID GEOMETRY

LEVEL 1

1. After being inflated, a spherical balloon has a radius of 9 inches. Which of the following is equal to the volume of the balloon, in cubic inches?

   A) 18π
   B) 81π
   C) 729π
   D) 972π

LEVEL 2

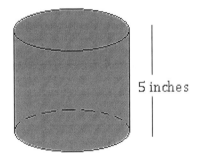

5 inches

2. * A can in the shape of a right circular cylinder is completely filled with soda as shown above. If the volume of the can is 8.45π cubic inches, what is the <u>diameter</u> of the base of the cylinder, in inches?

3. A box in the shape of a right rectangular prism has a volume of 252 cubic centimeters. If the dimensions of the box are 7 centimeters by 3 centimeters by w centimeters, what is the value of w ?

LEVEL 3

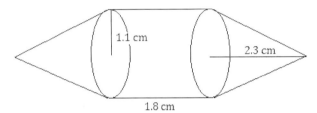

1.1 cm
2.3 cm
1.8 cm

4. * An NAID is a type of medication used to reduce inflammation. Suppose an NAID is created in pill form using two congruent right circular cones and a right circular cylinder with measurements shown in the figure above. Of the following, which is closest to the volume of the pill, in cubic centimeters?

   A) 2.91
   B) 5.83
   C) 6.84
   D) 12.67

5. A toy manufacturer makes spherical balls, each with a radius between 5.8 inches and 6.1 inches. What is one possible volume, rounded to the nearest cubic inch, of a toy ball produced by this manufacturer?

61

6. * Sydney has identical containers each in the shape of a cone with internal diameter 7 inches. She pours liquid from a two-gallon bottle into each container until it is full. If the height of liquid in each container is 10 inches, what is the largest number of full containers into which she can pour two gallons of liquid? (Note: There are 231 cubic inches in 1 gallon.)

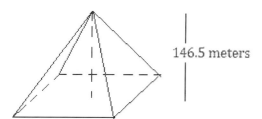

146.5 meters

7. * Before erosion and other factors had taken its toll, the *Great Pyramid of Giza* shown above had a square base and a volume of 2,592,276.48 cubic meters. What was the length of a side of the base, to the nearest meter?

LEVEL 4

8. The volume of right circular cylinder C is V cubic inches. Right circular cylinder D has twice the height and half the radius of right circular cylinder C. Which of the following expresses the volume of right circular cylinder D in terms of V ?

   A) $4V$
   B) $2V$
   C) V
   D) $\frac{V}{2}$

9. A storage facility stores containers shaped liked rectangular prisms that satisfy certain dimensional conditions. Specifically, the conditions state that the sum of the area of the base of the container (determined using the length and width of the container) and the height of the container cannot exceed 37 feet. If a certain container has a height of $24\frac{1}{2}$ feet, and a width that is half of its length, which of the following inequalities gives the possibilities for the length, L, in feet, of the container?

   A) $0 \le L \le 2\frac{1}{2}$
   B) $0 \le L \le 5$
   C) $0 \le L \le 7\frac{1}{2}$
   D) $0 \le L \le 10$

LEVEL 5

10. The surface area of a cube is $6\left(\frac{c}{4d}\right)^2$, where c and d are positive constants. Which of the following gives the area of one face of the cube?

   A) $\frac{4c}{d}$
   B) $\frac{c}{d}$
   C) $\frac{c^2}{4d^2}$
   D) $\frac{c^2}{16d^2}$

LESSON 21 – HEART OF ALGEBRA
INTERPRETING LINEAR EXPRESSIONS

LEVEL 1

$$s + b = 7$$

1. The equation above relates the number of strawberries, s, and the number of bananas, b, that are in Jonathon's fruit salad. What does the number 7 represent?

    A) The number of strawberries in the fruit salad
    B) The number of bananas in the fruit salad
    C) The total number of strawberries and bananas in the fruit salad
    D) The number of strawberries in the fruit salad for each banana in the fruit salad

2. Express Painting is hired to paint the walls in n rooms of equal size. Express Painting's fee, in dollars can be calculated by the expression $2nCh(\ell+w)$, where n is the number of rooms, C is the cost per square foot of the paint in dollars, ℓ is the length of each room in feet, w is the width of each room in feet, and h is the height of each room, in feet. If the customer chooses to use more expensive paint, which of the factors in the expression would change?

    A) n
    B) h
    C) $\ell+w$
    D) C

LEVEL 2

3. A cable company charges two types of fees: a one-time setup fee and a monthly service fee. The equation $C = 90x + 45$ represents the total cost, C, in dollars, for x months of cable service. What does 45 represent in the equation?

    A) The price of one typical month of service
    B) The total amount, in dollars, for cable access for one month
    C) The total amount, in dollars, for cable access for x months
    D) The cost of the setup fee, in dollars

LEVEL 3

4. The number of decks of cards, d, that a convenience store can sell per week at a price of p dollars is given by $d = 90 - 15p$. What is the meaning of the value 90 in this equation?

    A) 90 cents is the maximum that someone would pay for a deck of cards.
    B) 90 people per week would take a deck of cards for free.
    C) If the price of a deck of cards is decreased by 1 dollar, then 90 more people will make a purchase.
    D) If the price of a deck of cards is decreased by 90 cents, then 90 more people will make a purchase.

5. Premium Printing estimates the price of a printing job, in dollars, using the expression $2pt + 3$, where p is the number of printers and t is the total time, in minutes, needed to complete the job using p printers. Which of the following is the best interpretation of the number 2 in the expression?

A) Each printer prints for 2 minutes.
B) The price of the job increases by $2 every minute.
C) At least 2 printers are needed to complete the job.
D) Premium Printing charges $2 per minute for each printer.

$$L = 0.01x + 1.3$$

6. An entomologist uses the model above to estimate the length L of a certain species of insect, in centimeters, in terms of the insect's age x, in days. Based on the model, what is the estimated increase, in <u>millimeters</u>, of the insect's length each day? (1 centimeter = 10 millimeters)

A) 0.001
B) 0.01
C) 0.1
D) 1

7. The *femur*, or thigh bone, is the longest bone in the human body. The height of an adult male h, in inches, can be estimated by the linear function $h(x) = 1.88x + 32.01$, where x is the length of the adult male's femur, in inches. Which of the following statements is the best interpretation of the number 1.88 in this context?

A) The height of an adult male, in inches, whose femur is 32.01 inches long
B) The increase in the height of an adult male, in inches, that corresponds to a 1 inch increase in the length of the femur
C) The increase in the length of an adult male's femur, in inches, that corresponds to a 1 inch increase in the height of the adult male
D) The increase in the height of an adult male, in inches, that corresponds to a 32.01 inch increase in the length of the femur

LEVEL 4

8. While training for a competition, a swimmer decided to increase the number of laps he swam each day by a constant amount for 12 days. If he swam 14 laps on day 5 and 32 laps on day 11, which of the following best describes how the number of laps changed during his first 12 days of training?

   A) The swimmer increased the number of laps he swam by 1 per day.
   B) The swimmer increased the number of laps he swam by 3 per day.
   C) The swimmer increased the number of laps he swam by 1 every 3 days.
   D) The swimmer increased the number of laps he swam by 3 every 2 days.

.

9. At a factory, w workers are needed to build a appliances. If $w = 2a + 3$, how many additional workers are needed to make each additional appliance?

   A) None
   B) One
   C) Two
   D) Three

$$A = 20t + 100$$

10. The equation above gives the amount of money A deposited into a checking account, in dollars, after t months. Based on the equation, which of the following must be true?

   I. Each month, $20 is deposited into the account.
   II. $1 is deposited into the account every 20 months.
   III. The initial deposit into the account was $20.

   A) I only
   B) II only
   C) III only
   D) I and III only

LESSON 22 – PASSPORT TO ADVANCED MATH
EXPONENTS AND ROOTS

LEVEL 1

1. Which of the following is equivalent to $\dfrac{x^5 \cdot x^3}{x^8}$ for $x \neq 0$?

    A) 1
    B) x
    C) $x^{\frac{15}{8}}$
    D) $x^{\frac{5}{8}} \cdot x^{\frac{3}{8}}$

LEVEL 2

2. Which of the following is equal to $\dfrac{(xy)^7 (yz)^2}{y^9}$ for $y \neq 0$?

    A) 1
    B) xyz
    C) $x^7 z^2$
    D) $x^7 y^5 z^2$

LEVEL 3

3. Which of the following is equivalent to $\left(\dfrac{2}{3}\right)^3 \left(\dfrac{9}{4}\right)^2$?

    A) 0
    B) $\dfrac{2}{3}$
    C) 1
    D) $\dfrac{3}{2}$

4. If $(5^7)^x = (5^3)^5$, what is the value of x ?

    A) $\dfrac{1}{8}$
    B) $\dfrac{6}{7}$
    C) $\dfrac{15}{7}$
    D) 8

LEVEL 4

5. Which of the following is equivalent to $4^{\frac{5}{4}}$?

    A) $\sqrt[5]{4}$
    B) $\sqrt[4]{4}$
    C) $\sqrt{2}$
    D) $4\sqrt{2}$

6. Which of the following is equivalent to $7^{-\frac{11}{3}}$?

    A) $\sqrt[3]{7^{11}}$

    B) $\frac{1}{\sqrt[3]{7^{11}}}$

    C) $-\sqrt[3]{7^{11}}$

    D) $-\frac{1}{\sqrt[3]{7^{11}}}$

7. If $\sqrt[5]{k^3} \cdot \sqrt[3]{k^2} = k^m$ for all values of k, what is the value of m ?

8. If $x = 4\sqrt{3}$ and $3x = \sqrt{6y}$, what is the value of y ?

LEVEL 5

9. Which of the following is equivalent to
$$\frac{x^{-\frac{5}{2}} \cdot x^{-1}}{x^{-\frac{4}{3}}} ?$$

    A) $\sqrt[6]{x^{13}}$

    B) $\sqrt[13]{x^6}$

    C) $\frac{1}{\sqrt[6]{x^{13}}}$

    D) $\frac{1}{\sqrt[13]{x^6}}$

10. If $5a - 30b = 3$, what is the value of $\frac{4^a}{16^{3b}}$?

    A) 4^3

    B) $\sqrt{4^3}$

    C) $4^{\frac{3}{5}}$

    D) The value cannot be determined from the information given.

LESSON 23 – PROBLEM SOLVING
DATA ANALYSIS

LEVEL 3

1. The tables below give the distribution of the grades received by a class of 35 students on a math exam and a chemistry exam.

Math Exam			Chemistry Exam	
Grade	Frequency		Grade	Frequency
100	7		100	1
95	5		95	4
90	5		90	26
85	4		85	2
80	6		80	1
75	8		75	1

Which of the following is true about the data shown for these 35 students?

A) The standard deviation of grades on the math exam is larger.
B) The standard deviation of grades on the chemistry exam is larger.
C) The standard deviation of grades on the math exam is the same as that of the chemistry exam.
D) The standard deviation of grades on these two exams cannot be calculated with the data provided.

2. A data analyst was interested in the mean height of women in a small town. He randomly measured the heights of 200 women in that town, and found that the mean height of these women was 61 inches, and the margin of error for this estimate was 3 inches. The data analyst would like to repeat the procedure and attempt to reduce the margin of error. Which of the following samples would most likely result in a smaller margin of error for the estimated mean height of women in that same town?

A) 100 randomly selected people from the same town.
B) 100 randomly selected women from the same town.
C) 400 randomly selected people from the same town.
D) 400 randomly selected women from the same town.

3. A well-known animal organization wanted to analyze the opinions of residents in a certain city regarding the funding of an animal sanctuary within that city's limits. The organization surveyed a sample of 200 animal activists that live in the city. The survey showed that almost all those sampled fully supported the funding of the sanctuary. Which of the following is true about the organization's survey?

A) The survey should have consisted only of residents that are not animal activists.
B) The survey sample is biased because it is not representative of the residents living in the city.
C) The survey sample should have included more than 200 animal activists.
D) The survey shows that most of the residents in the city are in favor of funding the animal sanctuary.

4. A biologist was interested in the number of times a field cricket chirps each minute on a sunny day. He randomly selected 100 field crickets from a garden, and found that the mean number of chirps per minute was 112, and the margin of error for this estimate was 6 chirps. The biologist would like to repeat the procedure and attempt to reduce the margin of error. Which of the following samples would most likely result in a smaller margin of error for the estimated mean number of times a field cricket chirps each minute on a sunny day?

A) 50 randomly selected crickets from the same garden.
B) 50 randomly selected field crickets from the same garden.
C) 200 randomly selected crickets from the same garden.
D) 200 randomly selected field crickets from the same garden.

5. 1500 adults were selected at random from New York City and asked if they were satisfied with the condition of the roads in the city. Of those surveyed, 85 percent responded that they were not satisfied with the condition of the roads in the city. Based on the results of the survey, which of the following statements must be true?

I. If 1500 adults were surveyed from another city, 85 percent of them would report that they are not satisfied with the road conditions in the city.
II. Of all adults in New York City, 85 percent are not satisfied with the city's road conditions.
III. If another 1500 adults from New York City were surveyed, 85 percent of them would report that they are not satisfied with the road conditions in the city.

A) None
B) III only
C) II and III only
D) I, II, and III

6. A survey was conducted to determine how many single men in a large city wanted to get married. 250 single men who visited a local coffee shop on a Saturday were given the survey, and 20 men refused to respond. Which of the following factors makes it least likely that a reliable conclusion can be drawn about the percentage of single men in the city that want to get married.

A) Population size
B) Sample size
C) Where the survey was given
D) The number of people who refused to respond

7. A psychologist wanted to determine if there is an association between diet and stress levels for the population of middle aged women in New York. He surveyed a random sample of 1500 middle aged female New Yorkers and found substantial evidence of a positive association between diet and stress levels. Which of the following conclusions is well supported by the data?

A) A dietary change causes an increase in stress levels for middle aged women from New York.
B) An increase in stress levels causes middle aged women from New York to change their diets.
C) There is a positive association between diet and stress levels for middle aged women in New York.
D) There is a positive association between diet and stress levels for middle aged women in the world.

LEVEL 4

8. 15 women went on a 6 month long weight loss program. They recorded their weights, in pounds, before and after completing the program. The results can be seen in the dot plots below (all weights have been rounded to the nearest 10 pounds).

Weight before starting weight loss program

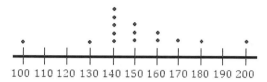

Weight after completing weight loss program

Let R_1 and σ_1 be the range and standard deviation, respectively, of the weights before beginning the weight loss program, and let R_2 and σ_2 be the range and standard deviation, respectively, of the weights after completing the weight loss program. Which of the following is true?

A) $R_1 = R_2$ and $\sigma_1 \neq \sigma_2$
B) $R_1 = R_2$ and $\sigma_1 = \sigma_2$
C) $R_1 < R_2$ and $\sigma_1 < \sigma_2$
D) $R_1 > R_2$ and $\sigma_1 > \sigma_2$

9. A survey was conducted at a local dog park to determine the mean number of pets per family in a neighborhood. The mean number of pets from the 35 respondents was found to be 2.8. Which of the following statements must be true?

A) The mean number of pets per family in the neighborhood is 2.8.
B) The sampling method is flawed and may produce a biased estimate of the mean number of pets per family in the neighborhood.
C) The sampling method is not flawed and is likely to produce an unbiased estimate of the mean number of pets per family in the neighborhood.
D) A determination about the mean number of pets per family in the neighborhood should not be made because the sample size is too small.

LEVEL 5

10. In a small city, a survey was taken to try to determine how much money families donate to charity each year. It was found that the median amount was $300 and the mean amount was $1700. Which of the following situations could explain the difference between the median and the mean gross income of families in the town?

A) There are a few families that donate much less money than the rest.
B) There are a few families that donate much more money than the rest.
C) All the families in the town donate approximately the same amount of money each year.
D) Many of the families donate between $300 and $1700 each year.

70

LESSON 24 – GEOMETRY
PARALLEL LINES AND SIMILARITY

LEVEL 2

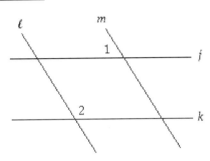

1. In the figure above, lines j and k are parallel and lines ℓ and m are parallel. If the measure of $\angle 1$ is $43°$, what is the measure of $\angle 2$? (Disregard the degree sign when gridding in your answer.)

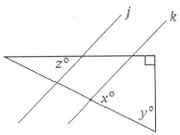

Note: Figure not drawn to scale.

3. In the figure above, lines j and k are parallel, $x = 100$, and $y = 35$. What is the value of z?

A) 35
B) 45
C) 55
D) 80

LEVEL 3

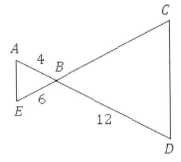

2. In the figure above, $AE \parallel CD$ and segment AD intersects segment CE at B. What is the length of segment CE?

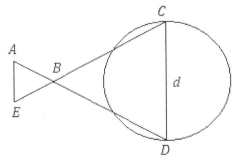

4. A surveyor wants to find the diameter, d, in meters, of a circular plot of land as represented in the sketch above. The lengths represented by AE, EB, BC, and BD on the sketch were determined to be 1200 meters, 1500 meters, 2500 meters, and 3100 meters, respectively. Segments AD and CE intersect at B, and $\angle EAB$ and $\angle CDB$ have the same measure. What is the value of d?

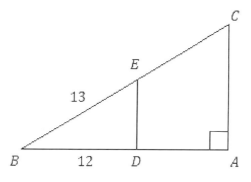

5. In the figure above, $\overline{DE}$ is parallel to $\overline{AC}$, D is the midpoint of $\overline{AB}$, $BD = 12$, and $BE = 13$. What is the length of $\overline{AC}$?

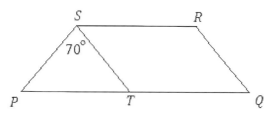

Note: Figure not drawn to scale.

6. In the figure above, $\overline{SR} \parallel \overline{PQ}$, $\overline{ST} \parallel \overline{RQ}$, $SP = ST$, and $m\angle PST = 70°$. What is $m\angle RST$? (disregard the degree symbol when gridding your answer.)

LEVEL 4

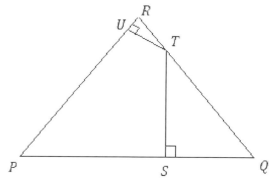

Note: Figure not drawn to scale.

7. Triangle PQR above is equilateral with $PQ = 44$. The ratio of ST to TU is $8:3$. What is the length of $\overline{SQ}$?

A) 6
B) 16
C) $16\sqrt{3}$
D) 32

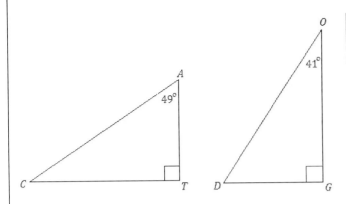

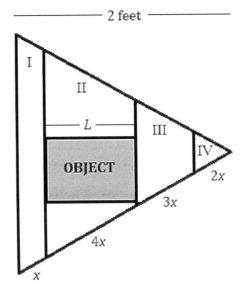

8. Triangles CAT and DOG are shown above. Which of the following is equal to the ratio $\frac{CT}{AT}$?

A) $\frac{DG}{DO}$

B) $\frac{DG}{OG}$

C) $\frac{OG}{DG}$

D) $\frac{DO}{OG}$

9. Tracy and Philip made a triangular shaped time capsule with 4 compartments as shown in the figure above. The total length is 2 feet. What is the maximum length L, in feet, of an object that can fit into compartment II?

LEVEL 5

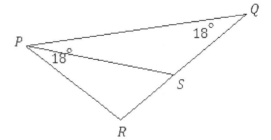

10. In the figure above, which of the following ratios has the same value as $\frac{PR}{PS}$?

A) $\frac{PQ}{QR}$

B) $\frac{PQ}{PR}$

C) $\frac{QR}{PQ}$

D) $\frac{QR}{PR}$

LESSON 25 – HEART OF ALGEBRA
MANIPULATING LINEAR EXPRESSIONS

LEVEL 1

1. If $2(x + y) = 7$, what is the value of $x + y$?

    A) $\frac{2}{7}$

    B) 2

    C) $\frac{7}{2}$

    D) 7

2. The formula below is used to compute C, the cost of goods sold, where B is the beginning inventory, P is the amount of inventory purchased, and E is the end inventory.

    $$C = B + P - E$$

    Which of the following correctly gives B in terms of C, P, and E ?

    A) $B = E - P - C$

    B) $B = C + P - E$

    C) $B = C + P + E$

    D) $B = C - P + E$

3. Which of the following inequalities is equivalent to $10x - 15y \leq 20$?

    A) $x - y \leq 2$

    B) $3x - 2y \leq 4$

    C) $2x - 3y \leq 4$

    D) $3y - 2x \leq 4$

4. If $9x - 27 = 72$, what is the value of $x - 3$?

LEVEL 2

$$0.7c = k$$

5. A 30% discount is given on a computer originally priced at c dollars. The new price is k and the relationship between c and k is given in the equation above. What is c in terms of k ?

    A) $c = 0.7k$

    B) $c = \frac{0.7}{k}$

    C) $c = \frac{k}{0.7}$

    D) $c = k - 0.7$

Questions 6 and 7 refer to the following information.

$$s = 127 + 2.37p$$

In the equation above, s represents the supply (the quantity a supplier is willing to make available), in units, of a certain item with a price of p dollars.

6. Which of the following expresses the price of the item in terms of the supply?

    A) $p = \frac{s + 127}{2.37}$

    B) $p = \frac{s - 127}{2.37}$

    C) $p = \frac{127 - s}{2.37}$

    D) $p = \frac{2.37}{s + 127}$

7.   * For which of the following prices will the supply be closest to 283 units?

A) $63
B) $65
C) $66
D) $67

LEVEL 3

Questions 8 - 10 refer to the following information.

Kelly is planning to add a garden to her backyard. The garden will be partitioned into rectangular blocks so that $3l + w = 16$, where l is the length and w is the width of each block, in feet. The lengths of all the blocks will be the same, and similarly for the widths.

8.   Which of the following expresses the length of a block in terms of its width?

A) $l = -\frac{1}{3}(16 + w)$

B) $l = -\frac{1}{3}(16 - w)$

C) $l = \frac{1}{3}(16 + w)$

D) $l = \frac{1}{3}(16 - w)$

LEVEL 4

9.   Kelly has decided that she would like the width of each block to be at least 7 feet and the length of each block to be at least 2 feet. Which of the following inequalities represents the set of all possible values for the length of the block that meets these requirements?

A) $0 \le l \le 3$
B) $2 \le l \le 3$
C) $3 \le l \le 7$
D) $l \ge 3$

LEVEL 5

10.   Kelly decides that she would like the total length of the garden to be 34 feet, with the length of each block between 3 and 4 feet. She also wants there to be 2 rows of blocks with an even number of blocks in each row. Which of the following must be the width of each block, in feet?

A) 3.4
B) 4.6
C) 5.8
D) 8.5

LESSON 26 – PASSPORT TO ADVANCED MATH
MANIPULATING NONLINEAR EXPRESSIONS

LEVEL 2

1. A rectangle has area A, length x and width y. Which of the following represents y in terms of A and x ?

   A) $y = \frac{A}{2x}$

   B) $y = \frac{A}{x}$

   C) $y = \frac{2A}{x}$

   D) $y = \frac{\sqrt{A}}{x}$

$$F(x) = |x^2 - 2| + 2$$

3. For what value of x is $F(x)$ equal to 0 ?

   A) 0

   B) 2

   C) $\sqrt{2}$

   D) There is no such value of x.

4. If $x \neq -\frac{3}{2}$, what is the value of
   $(10x + 15)\left(\frac{1}{2x+3}\right)$?

LEVEL 3

$$a = \frac{rP}{1 - (1 + r)^{-n}}$$

2. An *annuity* is a series of periodic payments that are received at a future date. In the formula above, a is the periodic payment on an annuity, P is the present value of the annuity, r is the interest rate per period, and n is the number of payment periods. Which of the following gives P in terms of a, r, and n.

   A) $P = ra$

   B) $P = (1 + r)^n a$

   C) $P = \frac{ra}{1-(1+r)^{-n}}$

   D) $P = a\frac{1-(1+r)^{-n}}{r}$

LEVEL 4

$$P = \frac{A}{A + N}$$

5. The formula above is used to compute the percentage P of people in a population that have anemia, where A is the number of people from the population that have anemia, and N is the number of people from the population that do not have anemia. Which of the following expresses the number of people that have anemia in terms of the other variables?

   A) $A = \frac{N}{P-1}$

   B) $A = \frac{N}{1-P}$

   C) $A = \frac{PN}{1-P}$

   D) $A = \frac{PN}{P-1}$

6. If $\frac{3}{x} = \frac{6}{x+9}$, what is the value of $\frac{x}{3}$?

    A) 3
    B) 6
    C) 9
    D) 12

7. A soda can manufacturer uses the formula $M = 2\pi r^2 n + \pi r h n$ to calculate the amount of material, M, needed to manufacture n cylindrical soda cans of height h and base radius r. Which of the following correctly expresses h in terms of M, n, and r ?

    A) $h = \frac{\pi r n}{M - 2\pi r^2}$
    B) $h = \frac{M - 2\pi r^2}{\pi r n}$
    C) $h = M - \frac{2r}{n}$
    D) $h = \frac{M}{\pi r n} - 2r$

LEVEL 5

8. If $k > -1$, which of the following is equivalent to $\dfrac{1}{\frac{1}{k+1} + \frac{1}{k+2}}$?

    A) $2k + 3$
    B) $k^2 + 3k + 2$
    C) $\frac{k^2 + 3k + 2}{2k + 3}$
    D) $\frac{2k + 3}{k^2 + 3k + 2}$

9. An encyclopedia salesman has a boxes, each containing 7 encyclopedias. After visiting b families and selling c encyclopedias to each of them, he has d encyclopedias remaining. Which of the following expresses b in terms of a, c, and d ?

    A) $\frac{7a - d}{c}$
    B) $\frac{7a + d}{c}$
    C) $\frac{7a}{c} - d$
    D) $\frac{7c - d}{a}$

10. The equation $\frac{36x^2 + 81x - 15}{kx - 7} = -3x - 5 - \frac{50}{kx - 7}$ is true for all values of $x \neq \frac{7}{k}$, where k is a constant. What is the value of $|k|$?

LESSON 27 – PROBLEM SOLVING
SCATTERPLOTS

LEVEL 1

Questions 1 - 4 refer to the following information.

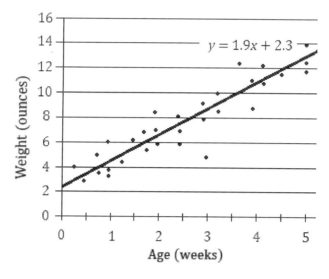

* The scatterplot above shows data collected on the age and weights of several kittens, and the line of best fit for the data is shown.

1. Which of the following is the best approximation to the weight, in ounces, of the youngest kitten for which there is a data point appearing in the scatterplot?

    A) 0.25
    B) 0.5
    C) 3
    D) 4

2. What is the age, in weeks, of the kitten represented by the data point that is farthest from the line of best fit?

    A) 3
    B) 4
    C) 5
    D) 6

LEVEL 2

3. * Based on the line of best fit, if a kitten is 6 weeks old, what is the predicted weight, in ounces, of the kitten?

    A) 11.8
    B) 13.7
    C) 14.65
    D) 15.6

LEVEL 3

4. Which of the following is the best interpretation of the slope of the line of best fit in the context of this problem?

   A) The predicted weight of a kitten that is 5 weeks old
   B) The predicted age of a kitten that was just born
   C) The predicted increase in weight, in ounces, for each week that a kitten ages
   D) The predicted increase in the age of a kitten needed to increase the kitten's weight by 1 ounce

5. Which of the following graphs best shows a strong positive association between x and y ?

A)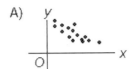

B)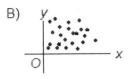

C)

D)

Questions 6 - 8 refer to the following information.

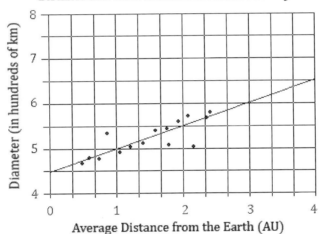

Distance and Mass of Asteroids in the Solar System

The scatterplot above shows the diameters of 15 asteroids, in hundreds of kilometers, with respect to their average distance from the earth in astronomical units (AU). The line of best fit is drawn.

6. A scientist has discovered a new asteroid about 2 AU from the Earth. According to the line of best fit, which of the following best approximates the diameter of the asteroid, in kilometers?

   A) 5.5
   B) 55
   C) 550
   D) 5500

7. 1 astronomical unit is equal to approximately 150 million kilometers. Which of the following gives the best estimate for the minimum possible distance, in millions of kilometers, between the largest and smallest asteroid whose data points appear in the scatterplot?

   A) 160
   B) 285
   C) 368
   D) 435

79

LEVEL 4

8. According to the scatterplot, which of the following statements is true about the relationship between an asteroid's average distance from the Earth and its size?

   A) The distance from an asteroid to the Earth is unrelated to its size.
   B) An asteroid that is further from the Earth is smaller than an asteroid that is closer to the Earth.
   C) An asteroid that is closer to the Earth is smaller than an asteroid that is further from the Earth.
   D) An asteroid that is further from the Earth is more likely to be larger than an asteroid that is closer to the Earth.

9. Which scatterplot shows a relationship that is appropriately modeled with the equation $y = ab^x$, where $a > 0$ and $0 < b < 1$?

A)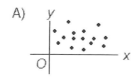

B)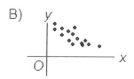

C)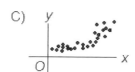

D)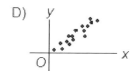

LEVEL 5

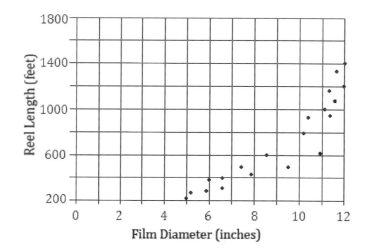

10. * The scatterplot above shows the lengths of several film reels, in feet, versus the diameters of the film on those reels, in inches. Of the following equations, which best models the data in the scatterplot?

   A) $y = -14.5x^2 - 112.3x + 430.2$
   B) $y = 14.5x^2 - 112.3x + 430.2$
   C) $y = -14.5x^2 + 112.3x - 430.2$
   D) $y = 14.5x^2 + 112.3x - 430.2$

LESSON 28 – COMPLEX NUMBERS
OPERATIONS

LEVEL 4

1. Which of the following is equal to i^{73} ?

    A) -1
    B) $-i$
    C) 1
    D) i

LEVEL 1

2. For $i = \sqrt{-1}$, the sum $(-3 + 2i) + (-5 - 7i)$ is equal to

    A) $-8 + 9i$
    B) $-8 - 5i$
    C) $2 + 9i$
    D) $2 - 5i$

3. If $(-3 + 5i) + (-2 - 7i) = a + bi$ and $i = \sqrt{-1}$, then what is the value of ab ?

LEVEL 2

4. When we subtract $7 - i$ from $-3 + 5i$ we get which of the following complex numbers?

    A) $-10 - 6i$
    B) $-10 + 6i$
    C) $4 + 4i$
    D) $4 - 4i$

5. Which of the following complex numbers is equal to $(5i^2 + 3i) - (2 - 7i)$?

    A) $-7 + 10i$
    B) $3 + 4i$
    C) $-3 - 4i$
    D) $7 - 10i$

6. Let a and b be real numbers and $i = \sqrt{-1}$. When we add $a + bi$ to $7 - 2i$, we get $-3 + 5i$. What is the value of b ?

LEVEL 3

7.   If $i = \sqrt{-1}$, which of the following complex numbers is equivalent to $(5 - 2i)(-2 + 7i)$?

A) $4 + 39i$
B) $4 - 39i$
C) $-10 + 14i$
D) $-10 - 14i$

$$i^3 + i^4 + i^5 + i^8$$

9.   The complex number expression above is equivalent to a real number a. What is the value of a ? (Note: $i = \sqrt{-1}$)

LEVEL 5

10.   If $(x - 3i)(5 + yi) = 28 - 3i$ then what is one possible value of $x + y$? (Note: $i = \sqrt{-1}$)

LEVEL 4

8.   Which of the following complex numbers is equivalent to $\frac{2-3i}{3+5i}$, where $i = \sqrt{-1}$?

A) $\frac{2}{3} + \frac{3}{5}i$
B) $\frac{2}{3} - \frac{3}{5}i$
C) $\frac{9}{34} + \frac{19}{34}i$
D) $-\frac{9}{34} - \frac{19}{34}i$

 **LESSON 29 – HEART OF ALGEBRA**
ADDITIONAL PRACTICE 2

LEVEL 1

1. If $y = \frac{3}{5}x + 1$ and $x = 20$, what is the value of $x - y$?

    A) 7
    B) 13
    C) 17
    D) 22

2. The formula $d = rt$ is used to find the distance an object travels over a span of time, t, at a constant rate, r. What is the time, t, expressed in terms of d and r ?

    A) $t = dr$
    B) $t = \frac{d}{r}$
    C) $t = \frac{r}{d}$
    D) $t = d - r$

LEVEL 2

3. Saline solution X contains 10% salt and saline solution Y contains 15% salt. Together, the 2 solutions contain a total of 5 ounces of salt. Which of the following equations models this relationship, where x is the number of ounces of saline solution X and y is the number of ounces of saline solution Y ?

    A) $0.1x + 0.15y = 5$
    B) $0.15x + 0.1y = 5$
    C) $10x + 15y = 5$
    D) $15x + 10y = 5$

$$A = 17t + 20$$

4. After making an initial deposit into a savings account in January, Candice proceeded to deposit a fixed amount of money into the same savings account each month, beginning in February. The equation above models the amount A, in dollars, that Candice has deposited after t monthly deposits. According to the model, how many dollars was Candice's initial deposit? (Disregard the $ sign when gridding your answer.)

LEVEL 3

5. The line k in the xy-plane contains points from each of Quadrants I and IV, but no points from Quadrants II and III. Which of the following must be true?

   A) The slope of line k is positive.
   B) The slope of line k is negative.
   C) The slope of line k is zero.
   D) The slope of line k is undefined.

6. Which of the following mathematical expressions is equivalent to the verbal expression "A number, k, doubled is 24 less than the product of k and 3"?

   A) $2k = 3k - 24$
   B) $k^2 = 3k - 24$
   C) $2k = 24 - 3k$
   D) $2k = 24 + 3k$

$$3(7x - 15) - (11 - 3x) = 4$$

7. What value of x satisfies the equation above?

8. When 11 is decreased by $3x$, the result is more than 5. What is the greatest possible integer value for x ?

LEVEL 4

9. In the xy-plane, the line determined by the points $(5a, 3)$ and $(15, a)$ passes through the origin. Which of the following could be the value of a ?

A) -3
B) 0
C) 2
D) 6

10. A person's weight on the Moon increases by approximately 1 pound for each 6 pound increase on Earth, and a person that weighs 102 pounds on Earth weighs approximately 17 pounds on the Moon. Which of the following equations best models the relationship between the weight of a person on Earth, e, and the weight of the person on the moon, m ?

A) $e = 6m$
B) $e = \frac{m}{6}$
C) $e = 6m + 102$
D) $e = \frac{m}{6} + 102$

11. * The monthly membership fee for a fitness center is \$49.99. The cost includes the usage of all equipment and classes with the exception of Pilates classes for which there is an additional fee of \$1.30 per class. For one month, Cindy's total membership fees were \$68.19. How many Pilates classes did Cindy take that month?

LEVEL 5

12. * The ionosphere is the layer of the earth's atmosphere that contains a high concentration of ions and free electrons and is able to reflect radio waves. It lies between about 40 to 620 miles above the Earth's surface. At a distance of 40 miles above the Earth's surface, the temperature is $-100°$ Fahrenheit, and at a distance of 600 miles above the Earth's surface, the temperature is $440°$ Fahrenheit. Given that the relationship between the distance above the Earth's surface, d, and the temperature, t, is linear, which of the following equations relates t and d ?

A) $d - t = 140$
B) $27d - 8t = 1880$
C) $d - 28t = 2840$
D) $27d - 28t = 3880$

LESSON 30 – PASSPORT TO ADVANCED MATH
ADDITIONAL PRACTICE 2

LEVEL 1

$$f(x) = 5x^2 - 7$$
$$g(x) = \frac{2}{3}x^3 + 5$$

1. The functions f and g are defined above. What is the value of $g(3) - f(1)$?

LEVEL 2

k	-2	2	3
$f(k)$	-7	1	3

2. The table above shows some values of the linear function f. Which of the following defines f ?

   A) $f(k) = k - 3$
   B) $f(k) = 2k - 3$
   C) $f(k) = 2k - 7$
   D) $f(k) = 4k - 1$

LEVEL 3

3. Which of the following is equivalent to $18a^4 - 32b^2$?

   A) $(9a^2 - 16b)(9a^2 + 16b)$
   B) $2(3a^2 - 4b)(3a^2 + 4b)$
   C) $2(6a^2 - 8b)(6a^2 + 8b)$
   D) $2(a^2 - 4b)(9a^2 + 4b)$

4. If $\sqrt{16} + \sqrt{k} = \sqrt{49}$, what is the value of k ?

   A) $\sqrt{3}$
   B) 3
   C) 9
   D) 3

$$\frac{x - y}{y} = z$$

5. In the equation above, if x and y are both negative, which of the following must be true?

    A) $z < -1$
    B) $z = -1$
    C) $z > -1$
    D) $z > 1$

LEVEL 4

6. If $xy = z$ and $x^2 + y^2 = w$, which of the following is equivalent to $w - 2z$?

    A) $(x + y)^2$
    B) $(x - y)^2$
    C) $(2x - 2y)^2$
    D) $2(x - y)^2$

7. A cone has volume V, height h, and base diameter d. Which of the following represents d in terms of V and h ?

    A) $d = 2\sqrt{V\pi h}$

    B) $d = \sqrt{\dfrac{V}{3\pi h}}$

    C) $d = \sqrt{\dfrac{3V}{\pi h}}$

    D) $d = 2\sqrt{\dfrac{3V}{\pi h}}$

$$x^3 + x^2 + x - 3 = (x - 1)(x^2 + kx + 3)$$

8. In the equation above, k is a constant. If the equation is true for all values of x, what is the value of k ?

LEVEL 5

9. The expression $\frac{7x-3}{x+4}$ is equivalent to which of the following?

   A) $\frac{7-3}{4}$

   B) $7 - \frac{3}{4}$

   C) $7 - \frac{3}{x+4}$

   D) $7 - \frac{31}{x+4}$

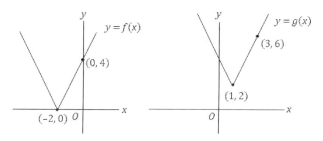

11. The figures above show the graphs of the functions f and g. The function f is defined by $f(x) = 2|x + 2|$ and the function g is defined by $g(x) = f(x + h) + k$, where h and k are constants. What is the value of $|h - k|$?

10. If $\frac{(x^a)^b x^c}{x^d} = x^4$ for all $x \neq 0$, which of the following must be true?

   A) $ab + c - d = 4$

   B) $\frac{ab+c}{d} = 4$

   C) $ab - cd = 4$

   D) $ab - c^d = 4$

$$\frac{7}{x+1} - \frac{3x-5}{(x+1)^2}$$

12. The expression above is equivalent to $\frac{ax+b}{(x+1)^2}$, where $x \neq -1$ and a and b are positive constants. What is the value of ab ?

LESSON 31 – PROBLEM SOLVING
ADDITIONAL PRACTICE 2

LEVEL 1

1. If a 6-pound quiche is cut into three equal pieces and each of those pieces is cut into four equal pieces, what is the weight, in ounces, of each piece of quiche?
(1 pound = 16 ounces)

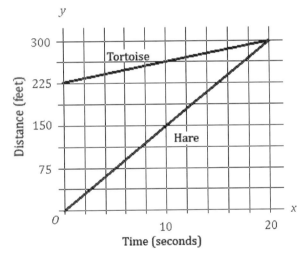

2. A tortoise and a hare had a race. The tortoise was given a head start and each ran at a constant rate. Both animals finished the race in 20 seconds, and so the result was a tie. The graph above shows the positions of the tortoise and the hare throughout the race. According to the graph, the tortoise was given a head start of how many feet?

LEVEL 2

3. * The distance traveled by Venus in one orbit around the Sun is about 420,000,000 miles. Venus makes one complete orbit around the sun in approximately seven Earth months. Of the following, which is the closest to the average speed of Venus, in miles per hour, as it orbits the Sun?

A) 60,000
B) 85,000
C) 100,000
D) 200,000

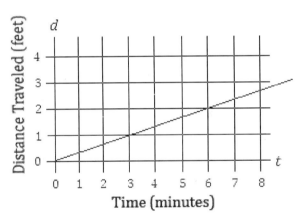

4. The graph above shows the distance travelled d, in feet, by a freight elevator t minutes after the freight elevator begins moving. Which of the following equations gives the correct relationship between d and t ?

A) $d = \frac{1}{3}t$
B) $d = 3t$
C) $d = t + 3$
D) $d = 3t + 3$

LEVEL 3

Age of 16 Tigers in a Sanctuary	
Age	Frequency
15	3
16	4
17	2
18	3
19	2
20	2

5.   * The table above shows the distribution of the ages of 16 tigers, in years, living in an animal sanctuary. Which of the following gives the correct order of the mean, median, and mode of the tigers' ages?

   A) median < mode < mean
   B) mean < mode < median
   C) mode < mean < median
   D) mode < median < mean

6.   Which of the following graphs best shows a strong negative association between x and y ?

A)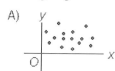
B)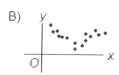

C)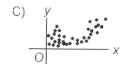
D)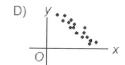

LEVEL 4

7.   A study was done on the flight speed of different types of birds in a sanctuary. A random sample of birds was selected and these birds were implanted with a tracker. 200 albatrosses were part of the sample, and it was observed that 25% of them flew faster than 75 miles per hour. Which of the following conclusions is best supported by the sample data?

   A) The average flight speed of all birds in the sanctuary is approximately 75 miles per hour.
   B) Most birds in the sanctuary cannot fly faster than 75 miles per hour.
   C) Approximately 25% of all albatrosses in the sanctuary can fly faster than 75 miles per hour.
   D) Approximately 25% of all birds in the sanctuary can fly faster than 75 miles per hour.

Questions 8 - 12 refer to the following information.

Machine	Depreciation Rate
Machine A	2.3%
Machine B	3.1%
Machine C	1.7%
Machine D	4.2%

To estimate the current value, V, of a machine, we use the formula $V = P\left(1 - \frac{r}{100}\right)^t$, where P is the original price of the machine, r is the approximate depreciation rate of the machine, and t is the age of the machine, in years. The table above gives the approximate depreciation rates for four different machines.

8. * Machine C is 3 years old and its original price was $5000. According to the information in the table, which of the following is closest to the current value of Machine C?

    A) $4951.28
    B) $4749.31
    C) $4549.27
    D) $4396.09

10. * A machine had an original price of $7500 four years ago, and its current value is $6612.36. The machine is most likely to be which of the following?

    A) Machine A
    B) Machine B
    C) Machine C
    D) Machine D

LEVEL 5

9. * If Machine A had an original price of $50,000, and now has a value of $47,750, which of the following will be closest to the age of Machine A, in years?

    A) 1
    B) 2
    C) 3
    D) 4

11. * If Machines A and B both have original values of $2000, which of the following will be closest to the difference, in dollars, of their prices when they are each 7 years old?

    A) $85
    B) $90
    C) $95
    D) $100

91

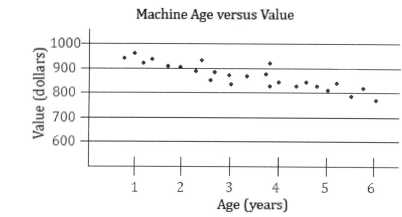

12. * The scatterplot above gives the age of 25 machines with original prices of $1000 plotted against their values. The depreciation rates of these machines are most likely closest to that of which of the following machines?

   A) Machine A
   B) Machine B
   C) Machine C
   D) Machine D

LESSON 32 – GEOMETRY AND COMPLEX NUMBERS
ADDITIONAL PRACTICE 2

LEVEL 1

1. In the standard (x, y) coordinate plane, point M with coordinates $(3, 7)$ is the midpoint of $\overline{PQ}$, and P has coordinates $(1, 9)$. What are the coordinates of Q ?

    A) $(5, 5)$
    B) $(-5, -5)$
    C) $(-1, 11)$
    D) $(4, 16)$

2. The circular base of a cone has a radius of 5 inches and the height of the cone is 3 inches. Which of the following is equal to the volume of the cone?

    A) 25
    B) 75
    C) 25π
    D) 75π

3. If $(7 - i) + (-1 + 3i) = a + bi$ and $i = \sqrt{-1}$, then what is the value of $\frac{a}{b}$?

LEVEL 2

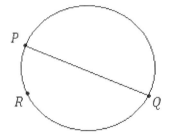

4. In the circle above, segment PQ is a diameter. If the length of arc $\overset{\frown}{PRQ}$ is 5π, what is the length of the <u>diameter</u> of the circle?

    A) 5
    B) 8
    C) 10
    D) 12

LEVEL 3

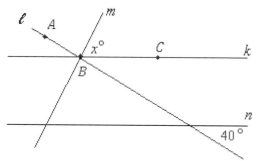

Note: Figure not drawn to scale.

5. In the figure above, line k is parallel to line n. If line m bisects angle ABC, what is the value of x ?

6. The height of a solid cone is 22 centimeters and the radius of the base is 15 centimeters. A cut parallel to the circular base is made completely through the cone so that one of the two resulting solids is a smaller cone. If the radius of the base of the small cone is 5 centimeters, what is the height of the small cone, in centimeters?

LEVEL 4

7. A cylindrical container contains various kinds of beans. The container is filled to the top with a liquid broth. The height of the container is 10 inches and the base of the container has a diameter of 5 inches. If exactly 182 cubic inches of broth is needed to completely fill the container, which of the following is the closest to the total volume of beans in the container, in cubic inches?

   A) 7
   B) 14
   C) 30
   D) 50

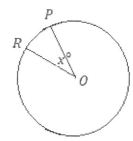

Note: Figure not drawn to scale.

8. In the figure above, O is the center of the circle, and the length of arc $\widehat{PR}$ is $\frac{2}{9}$ of the circumference of the circle. What is the value of x ?

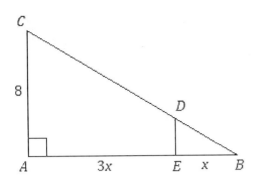

9. In the figure above, $\overline{AC} \parallel \overline{DE}$. What is the length of $\overline{DE}$?

10. If j and k are real numbers, $i = \sqrt{-1}$, and $(j - k) + 6i = 5 + ki$, what is jk ?

LEVEL 5

11. If a and b are real numbers, and $i = \sqrt{-1}$, which of the following must also be a real number?

    A) $(a + 2bi)^2$

    B) $(a - 2bi)(a + 2bi)$

    C) $ai^3 + 2bi^2$

    D) $\frac{a+2bi}{a-2bi}$

12. The lengths of the sides of a triangle are x, 3, and 5, where x is the shortest side. If the triangle is not isosceles, what is a possible value of x ?

LESSON 33 – HEART OF ALGEBRA
SOLVING LINEAR SYSTEMS OF EQUATIONS

LEVEL 1

$$y = 3 - x$$
$$2x = 6$$

1. Which of the following ordered pairs (x, y) satisfies the system of equations above?

    A) $(3, -1)$
    B) $(3, 0)$
    C) $(3, 1)$
    D) $(3, 2)$

LEVEL 2

2. If $x - y = 7$ and $\frac{x}{5} = 3$, what is the value of $x + y$?

    A) 18
    B) 20
    C) 21
    D) 23

LEVEL 3

$$\frac{2x}{3y} = 4$$
$$3(x - 2) = 6y$$

3. The system of equations above has solution (x, y). What is the value of x?

    A) $\frac{1}{2}$
    B) 1
    C) 3
    D) 6

$$6x - 3y = -21$$
$$5y - x = -10$$

4. What is the solution (x, y) to the system of equations above?

    A) $(3, -5)$
    B) $(5, -3)$
    C) $(-5, -3)$
    D) $(-3, 5)$

5. An adoption center has puppies and kittens. The adoption fee for a puppy is $250 and the adoption fee for a kitten is $150. One Saturday, a total of 20 puppies and kittens were adopted for a total cost of $3700. How many kittens were adopted on this particular Saturday?

 A) 5
 B) 7
 C) 11
 D) 13

LEVEL 4

$$5x - 3y = 4$$
$$5x + 4y = 7$$

6. * For the solution (x, y) to the system of equations above, what is the value of xy, rounded to the nearest tenth?

$$s = 21.7 + 5p$$
$$d = 35.3 - 3p$$

7. In the equations above, s and d represent the supply (the quantity supplied) and demand (the quantity demanded), in units, of a product with a price of p dollars. What is the price when the supply is equal to the demand?

8. * A Mexican restaurant sells quesadillas for $8.25 each and tacos for $4.50 each. The restaurant's revenue from selling a total of 89 quesadillas and tacos in eight hours was $498. How many quesadillas were sold during that eight-hour period?

LEVEL 5

$$5x + 3 + c = 2x$$
$$5y + 3 + d = 2y$$

9. In the equations above, c and d are constants. If d is c minus $\frac{1}{4}$, which of the following is true?

 A) x is y minus $\frac{1}{4}$.
 B) x is y minus $\frac{1}{12}$.
 C) x is y plus $\frac{1}{4}$.
 D) x is y plus $\frac{1}{12}$.

10. If $2x = 7 - 3y$ and $5y = 5 - 3x$, what is the value of x?

97

LESSON 34 – PASSPORT TO ADVANCED MATH
SOLVING QUADRATIC EQUATIONS

LEVEL 3

$$x^2 - 2x = 15$$

1. In the quadratic equation above, find the positive solution for x.

LEVEL 1

2. If $x > 0$ and $x^2 - 9 = 0$, what is the value of x ?

LEVEL 2

3. If $j > 0$ and $9j^2 - 36 = 0$, what is the value of j ?

LEVEL 3

$$g(x) = (x + 7)^2 - 25$$

4. Which of the following is a value of x that satisfies $g(x) = 0$?

   A) -12
   B) -7
   C) 0
   D) 2

LEVEL 4

5. What are the solutions to $7x^2 - 56x + 35 = 0$?

   A) $x = -28 \pm 35\sqrt{11}$
   B) $x = -28 \pm \sqrt{11}$
   C) $x = 4 \pm 35\sqrt{11}$
   D) $x = 4 \pm \sqrt{11}$

$$f(x) = \frac{1}{(x-7)^2 - 12(x-7) + 36}$$

6. For what value of x is the function f above undefined?

LEVEL 5

$$x^2 + \frac{4h}{3}x = 4k$$

7. In the quadratic equation above, h and k are constants. What are the solutions for x ?

A) $x = \frac{-2h \pm \sqrt{h^2 + 9k}}{3}$

B) $x = \frac{-2h \pm 2\sqrt{h^2 + 9k}}{3}$

C) $x = \frac{-2h \pm \sqrt{3h^2 + 9k}}{3}$

D) $x = -2h \pm \sqrt{h^2 + 3k}$

8. What is the sum of all values of p that satisfy $2p^2 - 27p + 13 = 0$?

9. If $2t^{-2} + 3t^{-1} - 2 = 0$, which of the following could be the value of t ?

A) $\frac{1}{3}$

B) $\frac{1}{2}$

C) 1

D) 2

$$ax^2 - 3x = b$$

10. In the equation above, a and b are constants. If the equation has 2 distinct real solutions, which of the following could be the value of ab ?

A) -4

B) -3

C) -2.25

D) -1.75

 **LESSON 35 – PROBLEM SOLVING**
PERCENTS

LEVEL 4

1. * Shelby bought a pair of jeans at a clothing store that gave a 40 percent discount off its original price. The total amount she paid to the cashier was x dollars, including a 7 percent sales tax on the discounted price. Which of the following represents the original price of the pair of jeans in terms of x ?

    A) $0.67x$
    B) $\dfrac{x}{0.67}$
    C) $(0.6)(1.07)x$
    D) $\dfrac{x}{(0.6)(1.07)}$

LEVEL 2

2. In January, Jane was able to type 30 words per minute. In February, she was able to type 42 words per minute. By what percent did Jane's speed increase from January to February?

    A) 12%
    B) 18%
    C) 30%
    D) 40%

3. * At Staten Island Middle School, approximately 5 percent of enrolled freshmen, 7 percent of enrolled sophomores, and 4 percent of enrolled juniors scored more than 80% on their State Exam in May 2016. If there were 276 freshmen, 365 sophomores, and 502 juniors at Staten Island Middle School in 2016, which of the following is closest to the total number of freshmen, sophomores, and juniors at Staten Island Middle School who scored more than 80% on their State Exam?

    A) 60
    B) 65
    C) 70
    D) 75

4. * Janice spent 22% of her 7-hour school day in her AP Calculus class. How many <u>minutes</u> of her school day were spent in AP Calculus?

    A) 1.54
    B) 24.3
    C) 46.97
    D) 92.4

5. * A geologist is studying igneous rock formations in two sections of a volcanic region. He observed that Section I had 26 percent more igneous rocks than Section II. Based on this observation, if Section I had 756 igneous rocks, then how many igneous rocks were in section II?

100

LEVEL 3

6. A family with an adjustable mortgage had to make a payment of $3217.53 per month. The interest rate has adjusted so that the family's monthly payment is now $3259.36. To the nearest tenth of a percent, by what percent did the amount of the family's mortgage payment increase?

   A) 1.1%
   B) 1.3%
   C) 1.5%
   D) 1.7%

7. An author sells his book for 95% more than the cost of printing the book. The author decides to throw a sale, and during the sale, he charges 45% more than the cost of printing the book. If the price of the book during the sale is $6.35, what is the price of the book, in dollars, when the book is not on sale? Round your answer to the nearest cent.

LEVEL 4

Questions 8 – 9 refer to the following information.

At the beginning of July, 58 percent of the animals in a shelter were dogs, and the rest were cats. By the end of July, 45 percent of the dogs and 63 percent of the cats were adopted.

8. * What percentage of the animals in the shelter were adopted? (Ignore the percent symbol when entering your answer.)

9. * What percentage of the animals that were adopted were cats? (Ignore the percent symbol when entering your answer.)

LEVEL 5

10. *If Ted's weight increased by 36 percent and Jessica's weight decreased by 22 percent during a certain year, the ratio of Ted's weight to Jessica's weight at the end of the year was how many times the ratio at the beginning of the year?

LESSON 36 – TRIGONOMETRY
RIGHT TRIANGLE TRIGONOMETRY

LEVEL 2

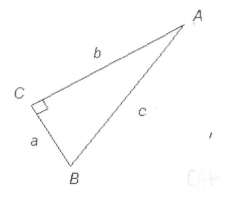

1. In the figure above, what is $\cos A$?

    A) $\dfrac{c}{b}$

    B) $\dfrac{a}{b}$

    C) $\dfrac{a}{c}$

    D) $\dfrac{b}{c}$

2. Let $x = \cos t$ and $y = \sin t$ for any real value t. Then $x^2 + y^2 =$

    A) -1
    B) 0
    C) 1
    D) It cannot be determined from the information given.

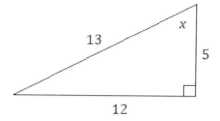

3. In the figure above, what is the value of $\tan x$?

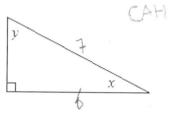

4. In the triangle above, the cosine of $x°$ is $\dfrac{6}{7}$. What is the tangent of $y°$?

    A) $\dfrac{\sqrt{13}}{7}$

    B) $\dfrac{\sqrt{13}}{6}$

    C) $\dfrac{6}{\sqrt{13}}$

    D) $\dfrac{7}{\sqrt{13}}$

5. In a right triangle, one angle measures $\theta°$, where $\cos\theta° = \dfrac{9}{11}$. What is $\sin((90 - \theta)°)$?

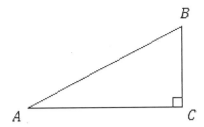

6. In the triangle above, the sine of A is 0.8. What is the cosine of B ?

LEVEL 5

8. Which of the following is equal to $\cos\left(\frac{\pi}{5}\right)$?

A) $-\cos\left(-\frac{\pi}{5}\right)$

B) $-\sin\left(\frac{\pi}{5}\right)$

C) $\sin\left(\frac{3\pi}{10}\right)$

D) $-\cos\left(\frac{3\pi}{10}\right)$

LEVEL 4

7. In triangles CAT and DOG, the measures of angles A and O are 90°. Triangle DOG is similar to triangle CAT, with vertices D, O, and G corresponding to vertices C, A, and T, respectively. $CA = 20$, $CT = 25$, and each side of triangle DOG is $\frac{2}{5}$ the length of the corresponding side of triangle CAT. What is the value of $\tan G$?

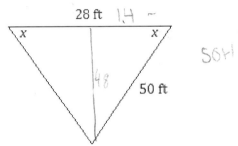

Note: Figure not drawn to scale.

9. * What is the value of $\sin x$ in the figure above?

10. The angle of elevation from the tip of the shadow of a 30 meter tall building to the top of the building has a cosine of $\frac{3}{7}$. What is the length of the shadow to the nearest meter?

103

LESSON 37 – HEART OF ALGEBRA
SETTING UP LINEAR SYSTEMS

LEVEL 3

1. A geologist has a collection of 55 rocks weighing a total of 15.34 pounds. Each of his igneous rocks weighs 0.12 pounds and each of his sedimentary rocks weighs 0.35 pounds. If the geologist has g igneous rocks and s sedimentary rocks, which of the following systems of equations can be used to find the number of igneous rocks in the geologist's collection?

A) $g + s = 15.34$
   $0.12g + 0.35s = 55$

B) $g + s = 15.34$
   $0.35g + 0.12s = 55$

C) $g + s = 55$
   $0.12g + 0.35s = 15.34$

D) $g + s = 55$
   $0.35g + 0.12s = 15.34$

2. A grocery store sells whole milk and low-fat milk in half-gallon containers. A half-gallon of whole milk costs $3.75 and a half-gallon of low-fat milk costs $4.25. During a typical week, 128 half-gallon cartons of milk were sold bringing in total revenue of $516 to the grocery store. Which of the following systems of equations could be used to find the number of half-gallon cartons of whole milk, W, and the number of half-gallon cartons of low-fat milk, L, that were sold at the grocery store?

A) $W + L = 128$
   $3.75W + 4.25L = 516$

B) $W + L = 516$
   $3.75W + 4.25L = 128$

C) $W + L = 128$
   $4.25W + 3.75L = 516$

D) $W + L = 128$
   $(3.75W)(4.25L) = 516$

LEVEL 4

3. A high school has a budget of $740 for math text books. Each geometry book costs $35 and each algebra book costs $40. The school needs to order at least 18 books. Which of the following systems of inequalities represents this situation in terms of x and y, where x is the number of geometry books ordered and y is the number of algebra books ordered?

A) $x + y \geq 18$
   $35x + 40y \geq 740$

B) $x + y \geq 18$
   $35x + 40y \leq 740$

C) $x + y \leq 18$
   $35x + 40y \geq 740$

D) $x + y \leq 18$
   $35x + 40y \leq 740$

4. A grocer plans to order a maximum of 200 cans of beans. Black beans cost the grocer $0.35 per can and kidney beans cost the grocer $0.42 per can. If the grocer can spend no more than $75 in total and the grocer orders b cans of black beans and k cans of kidney beans, which of the following systems best represents the constraints on b and k ?

A) $b + k \leq 0.77$
   $0.35b + 0.42k \leq 200$

B) $b + k \leq 200$
   $0.35b + 0.42k \leq 75$

C) $b + k \leq 0.77$
   $0.35b + 0.42k > 200$

D) $b + k \leq 200$
   $0.35b + 0.42k \geq 75$

5. Containers of two different weights are loaded into a storage facility. Each of the lighter containers weighs 32 pounds, and each of the heavier containers weighs 61 pounds. Let x be the number of lighter containers in the storage facility and let y be the number of heavier containers in the storage facility. The storage facility has a maximum weight limit of 2000 pounds and it has enough space for a total of 42 containers. Which of the following systems of inequalities represents this relationship?

A) $\begin{cases} x + y \leq 2000 \\ 32x + 61y \leq 42 \end{cases}$

B) $\begin{cases} x + y \leq 42 \\ 32x + 61y \leq 2000 \end{cases}$

C) $\begin{cases} \frac{x}{32} + \frac{y}{61} \leq 2000 \\ x + y \leq 42 \end{cases}$

D) $\begin{cases} x + y \leq 2000 \\ 32x + 61y \leq 2000 \end{cases}$

6. John is planning to spend his Sunday playing video games at an arcade. Each classic arcade game costs \$0.75 per game, and each new arcade game costs \$2.25 per game. John would like to play at least 60 games and he can spend at most \$75. If c represents the number of classic video games played and n represents the number of new video games played, which of the following systems of inequalities represents the situation?

A) $\begin{cases} c + n \leq 60 \\ 0.75c + 2.25n \geq 75 \end{cases}$

B) $\begin{cases} c + n \leq 60 \\ 2.25c + 0.75n \geq 75 \end{cases}$

C) $\begin{cases} c + n \geq 60 \\ 0.75c + 2.25n \leq 75 \end{cases}$

D) $\begin{cases} c + n \geq 60 \\ 2.25c + 0.75n \leq 75 \end{cases}$

LEVEL 5

7. A movie is available on DVD and Blue-ray. The box for the DVD has a volume of 260 cubic centimeters and the box for the Blu-ray has a volume of 230 cubic centimeters. An order of DVDs and Blue-rays was shipped to a warehouse. The total volume shipped was 12,010 cubic centimeters, and the shipment contained 50 copies of the movie. Which of the following systems of equations can be used to determine the number of DVDs, d, and the number of Blue-rays, b, that were shipped to the warehouse?

A) $d - b = 50$
   $245(d + b) = 12{,}010$

B) $d - b = 50$
   $260d + 230b = 12{,}010$

C) $50 - d = b$
   $230d + 260b = 12{,}010$

D) $50 - b = d$
   $260d + 230b = 12{,}010$

8. A real estate agent was selling all the houses on a block. The basic house was being sold for \$800,000 and the house with upgrades was being sold for \$925,000. Her goal was to sell at least 15 of the homes within 6 months. She didn't meet her goal, but she did sell houses that totaled over \$10,000,000. Which of the following systems of inequalities describes x, the possible number of standard houses and y, the possible number of upgraded houses?

A) $x + y > 15$
   $800{,}000x + 925{,}000y > 10{,}00{,}0000$

B) $x + y > 15$
   $800{,}000x + 925{,}000y < 10{,}00{,}0000$

C) $x + y < 15$
   $800{,}000x + 925{,}000y > 10{,}00{,}0000$

D) $x + y < 15$
   $800{,}000x + 925{,}000y < 10{,}00{,}0000$

9. A film producer needs to hire at least 20 crew members for a project. The crew will be made up of electricians, who must be paid $200 per day, and assistants, who must be paid $120 per day. The project's budget for paying the crew members is $3200 per day. At least 2 electricians and 3 assistants are needed. Which of the following systems of inequalities represents the given conditions if x is the number of electricians and y is the number of assistants?

A) $200x + 120y \leq 3200$
   $x + y \geq 20$
   $x \leq 2$
   $y \leq 3$

B) $200x + 120y \geq 3200$
   $x + y \leq 20$
   $x \geq 2$
   $y \geq 3$

C) $200x + 120y \leq 3200$
   $x + y \geq 20$
   $x \geq 2$
   $y \geq 3$

D) $200x + 120y \leq 3200$
   $x + y \leq 20$
   $x \leq 2$
   $y \leq 3$

10. A printer is purchasing paper and ink from its supplier. The supplier will deliver at most 250 pounds per shipment. Each ream of paper weighs 20 pounds and each ink cartridge weighs $\frac{1}{3}$ of a pound. The printer wants to purchase at least twice as many ink cartridges as reams of paper. Let r represent the number of reams of paper, and let c represent the number of ink cartridges, where r and c are positive integers. Which of the following systems of inequalities best represents this situation?

A) $20r + \frac{1}{3}c \leq 250$
   $2r \leq c$
   $r > 0$
   $c > 0$

B) $20r + \frac{1}{3}c \leq 250$
   $2r \geq c$
   $r > 0$
   $c > 0$

C) $\frac{1}{3}r + 20c \geq 250$
   $2r \leq c$
   $r > 0$
   $c > 0$

D) $\frac{1}{3}r + 20c \geq 250$
   $2r \geq c$
   $r > 0$
   $c > 0$

LESSON 38 – PASSPORT TO ADVANCED MATH
NONLINEAR SYSTEMS OF EQUATIONS

LEVEL 1

$$y = x^2$$
$$y = x$$

1. Which value is an x-coordinate of a solution to the system of equations above?

   A) -2
   B) -1
   C) 1
   D) 2

LEVEL 2

$$x = \frac{y - 4}{2}$$
$$y = x^2 + 4x - 11$$

2. Which of the following ordered pairs (x, y) satisfies both of the above equations?

   A) $(-2, 0)$
   B) $(-5, 6)$
   C) $(3, 10)$
   D) $(2, 1)$

LEVEL 3

3. In the xy-plane, the graph of $y = 5x^2 - 9x$ intersects the graph of $y = 2x$ at the points $(0, 0)$ and $(c, 2c)$, where $c \neq 0$. What is the value of c ?

LEVEL 4

$$x = y^2$$
$$5x + 12 = 2(y + 6)$$

4. If (x, y) is a solution of the system of equations above and $y > 0$, what is the value of $\frac{y}{x}$?

   A) 1.5
   B) 2
   C) 2.5
   D) 3

$$x + y^2 = 3$$
$$3y - x = 7$$

5. Which value is an x-coordinate of a solution to the system of equations above?

   A) -1
   B) 0
   C) 1
   D) 22

107

$$y = ax^2 - b$$
$$y = 8$$

6. In the system of equations above, a and b are nonzero constants. For which of the following values of a and b does the system of equations have exactly one real solution?

    A) $a = -2, b = -8$
    B) $a = 2, b = -6$
    C) $a = 2, b = -4$
    D) $a = 2, b = 4$

LEVEL 5

$$y = x^2 + 5x + 6$$
$$7x + 4 - y = 0$$

7. How many solutions are there to the system of equations above of the form (x, y), with x a real number?

    A) 0
    B) 1
    C) 2
    D) More than 2

$$y = x^2 + x + 12$$
$$y = 7x + 3$$

8. What is the y-coordinate of the point of intersection of the graphs of the equations above?

$$y = 3 - 2x$$
$$y = x^2 - 9x + 3$$

9. If the ordered pair (x, y) satisfies the system of equations above, and $x \neq 0$, what is one possible value of $|xy|$?

$$y = (2 - x)(3x - 1)$$
$$x = 2y + 5$$

10. * How many ordered pairs (x, y) satisfy the system of equations shown above?

LESSON 39 – PROBLEM SOLVING
PROBABILITY

LEVEL 1

Instruments Played by Children in a Community

Instrument	Piano	Guitar	Drums	Violin	Trumpet
Number of children who play instrument	3	7	15	1	4

1. * The instruments that each of 30 children in a community can play is shown in the chart above. Assume that each child plays exactly one instrument. If a child is chosen at random, which of the following is closest to the probability that the child can play the trumpet?

    A) 0.03
    B) 0.13
    C) 0.23
    D) 0.5

LEVEL 3

	Less than 2.5	Between 2.5 and 3.5	Greater than 3.5	Total
School A	272	117	36	425
School B	146	308	121	575
Total	418	425	157	1000

2. * The data in the table above categorizes the GPAs of the students from two high schools. If a student with a GPA between 2.5 and 3.5 is chosen at random, what is the probability that the student goes to school B?

Questions 3 - 5 refer to the following information.

A survey was conducted among a randomly chosen sample of 100 males and 100 females to gather data on pet ownership. The data are shown in the table below.

	Has pets	Does not have pets	Total
Men	75	25	100
Women	63	37	100
Total	138	62	200

3. According to the table, what is the probability that a randomly selected person has pets?

   A) $\frac{3}{8}$

   B) $\frac{25}{46}$

   C) $\frac{69}{100}$

   D) $\frac{3}{4}$

5. * According to the table, what is the probability that a randomly selected person with pets is female?

4. According to the table, what is the probability that a randomly selected man does not have pets?

Questions 6 - 7 refer to the following information.

Number of Students by Quiz and Grade						
1990	0%	25%	50%	75%	100%	Total
Quiz 1	2	4	6	10	8	30
Quiz 2	2	8	9	6	5	30
Quiz 3	1	3	5	9	12	30
Total	5	15	20	25	25	90

30 students in a math class took 3 short quizzes during the school year. Each quiz consisted of 4 questions, each question contributing to 25% of the quiz grade. The number of students receiving each of the 5 possible grades on each quiz is shown in the table above.

6. What was the mean grade of the students on the second quiz? (Disregard the percent symbol when gridding your answer.)

LEVEL 4

7. Assume that no student received the same grade on two different quizzes. If a student is selected at random, what is the probability that that student received a score of 100% on the first or third quiz, assuming that the student received a grade of 100% on one of the three quizzes?

111

LEVEL 5

Questions 8 - 10 refer to the following information.

Average Number of Meals Per Day

	Less than 3	3 to 5	More than 5	Total
Active	21	56	123	200
Inactive	56	96	48	200
Total	77	152	171	400

The table above was created by a health and fitness researcher studying the number of meals active and inactive people eat per day.

8. If a person is chosen at random from those who eat at least 3 meals per day, what is the probability that the person is active?

   A) $\frac{7}{19}$

   B) $\frac{179}{400}$

   C) $\frac{179}{323}$

   D) $\frac{179}{200}$

9. What is the probability that a randomly selected inactive person eats exactly 2 meals per day?

   A) $\frac{7}{75}$

   B) $\frac{7}{25}$

   C) $\frac{56}{77}$

   D) Cannot be determined from the given information

10. What is the probability that a randomly selected person is inactive or eats no more than 5 meals per day?

LESSON 40 – GEOMETRY
POLYGONS

LEVEL 1

1. What is the area of a rectangle, in square centimeters, that has a perimeter of 100 centimeters and a length of 20 centimeters?

LEVEL 2

2. The perimeter of a rectangle with side lengths a and b is $P = 2a + 2b$. Each side of Rectangle I has a length that is 3 times the length of Rectangle II. The perimeter of Rectangle II is what fraction of the perimeter of Rectangle I?

LEVEL 3

3. A rectangle has a perimeter of 100 feet. What is the area of the rectangle, in square feet?

   A) 200
   B) 400
   C) 600
   D) Cannot be determined from the given information

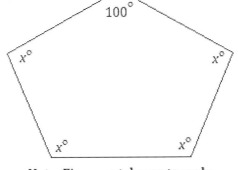

Note: Figure not drawn to scale.

4. In the figure above, what is the value of x ?

   A) 100
   B) 105
   C) 108
   D) 110

5. The measure x, in degrees, of an exterior angle of a regular polygon is related to the number of sides, n, of the polygon by the formula $nx = 360$. If the measure of an exterior angle of a regular polygon is less than 50°, what is the least number of sides it can have?

LEVEL 4

6. A line segment is drawn from the center of a 12-sided regular polygon to each vertex of the polygon forming 12 isosceles triangles. What is the measure of a base angle of one of these triangles? (Disregard the degree symbol when gridding your answer.)

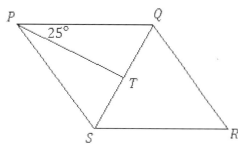

7. In the rhombus shown above, $m\angle QPT = 25°$ and T splits $\overline{QS}$ into two equal pieces. What is $m\angle QSR$? (Disregard the degree symbol when gridding your answer.)

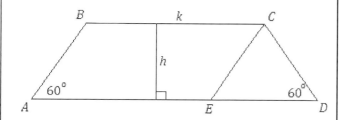

8. In the figure above, $ABCE$ is a parallelogram. In terms of h, how much smaller is the area of this parallelogram than the area of trapezoid $ABCD$?

A) $\frac{1}{3}h^2$

B) $\frac{2}{3}h^2$

C) $\frac{\sqrt{3}}{3}h^2$

D) $\frac{2\sqrt{3}}{3}h^2$

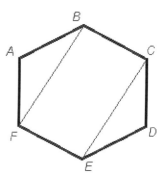

9. * In the figure above, $ABCDEF$ is a regular hexagon and $CD = 6$. What is the perimeter of rectangle $BCEF$ to the nearest tenth?

10. * The head of a copper "hexagon head screw bolt" (one cross section of which is shown above) has the shape of a cylinder with a hole shaped like a regular hexagon. The cylindrical head is 2 cm thick with a base diameter of 3 cm. The hexagonal hole is only half the thickness of the entire head, and each side of a hexagonal cross section has a length of 1 cm. Given that the density of copper is 8.96 grams per cubic cm, and density is mass divided by volume, find the mass of the head to the nearest gram.

114

LESSON 41 – HEART OF ALGEBRA
ADVANCED LINEAR SYSTEMS

LEVEL 4

$$2x + 8y = 6$$
$$3x + 12y = 9$$

1. Which of the following statements is true about the system of equations shown above?

    A) The two equations represent parallel but distinct lines.
    B) The two equations represent the same line.
    C) The graphs of the two equations intersect at a single point.
    D) The graphs of the two equations intersect at 2 points.

LEVEL 5

$$y \leq 2x + 2$$
$$y \geq -3x - 3$$

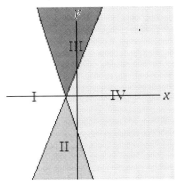

2. A system of inequalities and a graph are shown above. Which section or sections of the graph could represent all the solutions to the system?

    A) Section I
    B) Section IV
    C) Sections II and III
    D) Sections I, II, and IV

LEVEL 2

$$y > 5x + 2$$
$$y - x \leq 3$$

3. Which of the following ordered pairs (x, y) satisfies the system of inequalities above?

    A) $(5, 2)$
    B) $(0, 4)$
    C) $(-1, 1)$
    D) $(1, -1)$

LEVEL 3

$$y < x + k$$
$$y > m - x$$

4. In the xy-plane, $(0,0)$ is a solution to the system of inequalities above. Which of the following relationships between k and m must be true?

    A) $k = -m$
    B) $k > m$
    C) $k < m$
    D) $|k| < |m|$

$$x + y < 1$$
$$3y > 2$$

5. Which of the following consists of the x-coordinates of all the points that satisfy the system of inequalities above?

    A) $x < \frac{1}{3}$
    B) $x < 1$
    C) $x > \frac{1}{3}$
    D) $x > 1$

LEVEL 4

$$16x - ky = 8$$
$$kx + 4y = 3$$

6. In the system of equations above, k is a constant and x and y are variables. For what real value of k will the system of equations have no real solution?

   A) -8
   B) 0
   C) 8
   D) There is no such value of k.

$$y + 15x = 2$$
$$5y + 3y = 10$$

7. How many solutions (x, y) are there to the system of equations above?

   A) None
   B) One
   C) Two
   D) More than two

LEVEL 5

$$5x + 15y = 23$$
$$cx + dy = 49$$

8. In the system of equations above, c and d are constants. If the system has infinitely many solutions, what is the value of $\frac{c}{d}$?

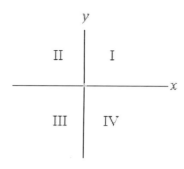

9. If the system of inequalities $y > 4x + 1$ and $y \leq -\frac{1}{2}x - 2$ is graphed in the xy-plane above, which quadrants contain no solutions to the system?

   A) Quadrant II
   B) Quadrant III
   C) Quadrants I and IV
   D) There are solutions in all four quadrants.

$$y \geq -7x + 1045$$
$$y \geq 4x$$

10. In the xy-plane, if a point with coordinates (a, b) lies in the solution set of the system of inequalities above, what is the minimum possible value of b?

LESSON 42 – PASSPORT TO ADVANCED MATH
GRAPHS OF PARABOLAS

LEVEL 3

1. Let the function f be defined by $f(x) = 3(x - 2)^2 + 1$. For what value of x will the function f have its minimum value?

    A) -3
    B) -2
    C) 2
    D) 3

LEVEL 4

2. Let the function f be defined by
    $f(x) = -7x^2 + 3x + 1$. For what value of x will the function f have its maximum value?

LEVEL 3

$$y = x^2 - 12x + 27$$

3. The equation above represents a parabola in the xy-plane. Which of the following equivalent forms of the equation displays the x-intercept(s) of the parabola as constants or coefficients?

    A) $y - 27 = x^2 - 12x$
    B) $y + 9 = (x - 6)^2$
    C) $y = x(x - 12) + 27$
    D) $y = (x - 3)(x - 9)$

4. In the xy-plane, the parabola with equation $y = (x + 7)^2$ intersects the line with equation $y = 9$ at two points, P and Q. What is the length of $\overline{PQ}$?

LEVEL 4

5. The graph of the function h defined by $h(x) = (x + 5)(x + 6)$ in the xy-plane is a parabola. Which of the following intervals contains the x-coordinate of the vertex of the graph of h ?

    A) $-7 < x < -5$
    B) $-5 < x < -2$
    C) $-2 < x < 2$
    D) $2 < x < 6$

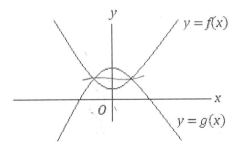

6. The functions f and g, whose graphs are shown above, are defined by $f(x) = 4x^2 + 1$ and $g(x) = -4x^2 + 3$. The graphs of f and g intersect at the points $(a, 2)$ and $(-a, 2)$. Given that $a > 0$, what is the value of a ?

117

LEVEL 5

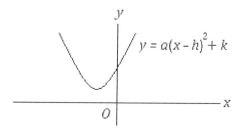

7. The vertex of the parabola in the xy-plane above is (h, k). Which of the following is true about the parabola with the equation $y = -ax^2 + k$?

A) The parabola opens upward and the vertex is $(0, k)$.
B) The parabola opens downward and the vertex is $(0, k)$.
C) The parabola opens upward and the vertex is $(0, -k)$.
D) The parabola opens downward and the vertex is $(0, -k)$.

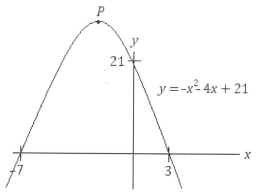

8. Which of the following is an equivalent form of the function f whose graph is shown above in the xy-plane, from which the coordinates of vertex P can be identified as constants in the equation?

A) $f(x) = -(x - (-2))^2 + 25$
B) $f(x) = -x(x + 2) + 21$
C) $f(x) = (x + 7)(x - 3)$
D) $f(x) = (x + 7)(3 - x)$

$$y = p(x - 3)(x + 7)$$

9. In the quadratic equation above, p is a nonzero constant. The graph of the equation in the xy-plane is a parabola with vertex (h, k). What is the value of $\sqrt{-\dfrac{k}{p}}$?

10. * An arrow is launched upward with an initial speed of 30 m/s (meters per second). The equation $v^2 = v_0^2 - 2gh$ describes the motion of the arrow, where v_0 is the initial speed of the arrow, v is the speed of the arrow as it is moving up in the air, h is the height of the arrow above the ground, t is the time elapsed since the arrow was projected upward, and g is the acceleration due to gravity (approximately 9.8 m/s²). What is the maximum height from the ground the arrow will rise to the nearest meter?

LESSON 43 – PROBLEM SOLVING
GROWTH

LEVEL 3

Questions 1 - 2 refer to the following information.

Grant invests in a bond that earns 4.2 percent interest compounded annually. His initial deposit was $700, and he uses the expression $700(1 + r)^t$ to find the value of the bond after t years.

1. What is the value of r in the expression?

2. * Grant's cousin Tana opened a savings account that earns 3.3 percent interest compounded annually. Tana also made an initial investment of $700 at the same time that Grant made his initial investment of $700. After 5 years, how much more money will Grant's investment have earned than Tana's initial investment? (Round your answer to the nearest cent and ignore the dollar sign when gridding your response.)

LEVEL 4

3. The value of an amethyst is expected to increase by 3.5 percent from one year to the next beginning in the year 2018. What type of relationship should be expected between the age of the amethyst and the amethyst's value?

    A) Linear relationship
    B) Quadratic relationship
    C) Cubic relationship
    D) Exponential relationship

Time (years)	Bullfrog Population
0	100
1	150
2	224
3	334
4	500
5	747

4. 100 bullfrogs were introduced into a small pond. The population of the bullfrogs in the pond, starting with the time they were introduced, is estimated over the course of 5 years as shown in the following table. Which of the following best describes the relationship between time and the estimated population of bullfrogs during the 5 years?

    A) Decreasing Linear
    B) Increasing Linear
    C) Exponential Decay
    D) Exponential Growth

5. The 60 plus population in New York City has grown at an average rate of approximately 3.2% per year from 2000 to 2010 with about 1.4 million people aged 60 and above living in New York City in 2000. Which of the following functions represents the 60 plus population in New York City, P, in millions of people, t years after 2000, with $0 \le t \le 10$?

A) $P(t) = 1.032t + 1.4$
B) $P(t) = 1.32t + 1.4$
C) $P(t) = 1.4(1.032)^t$
D) $P(t) = 1.4(1.32)^t$

6. * A rare gem is worth $1500 today. A jeweler believes that the gem will increase in value by 8% each month for the next eight months. The jeweler uses the equation $A = 1500(r)^t$ to model the value, A, of the gem after t months. To the nearest dollar, what does the jeweler believe the gem will be worth at the end of eight months?

LEVEL 5

7. * Sarah made an investment of D dollars on January 1, 2010. The amount of money in the account tripled each year until the investment was worth 1000 dollars on January 1, 2013. What is the value of D, to the nearest dollar?

8. * Satellites can be powered by the nuclear energy derived from radioactive isotopes. The table below shows the approximate output, in watts, of the radioactive power supply for a satellite at 10 day intervals following the activation of the power supply.

Days after activation	Output (watts)
0	30
10	29.11
20	28.25
30	27.42
40	26.6

The output, in watts, of the radioactive power supply t days after activation is modeled by the function $W = 30k^{-0.003t}$. If W approximates the values in the table to within 0.1 watts, what is the value of k, rounded to the nearest tenth?

Questions 9 - 10 refer to the following information.

An environmentalist is monitoring the mosquito population in an environment which currently contains 200 million mosquitos. The number of mosquitos, in millions, that the environmentalist expects each month, x_{next}, can be estimated from the number of mosquitos, in millions, the previous month, x_{previous}, by the following equation.

$$x_{\text{next}} = x_{\text{previous}} + 0.3x_{\text{previous}}\left(1 - \frac{x_{\text{previous}}}{E}\right)$$

The constant E in the formula is the number of mosquitos, in millions, that can be supported by the environment.

9. * If the environment can support 700 million mosquitos, what will be the number of mosquitos, in millions, three months from now? (Round your answer to the nearest whole number.)

10. The environmentalist suggests restricting the environment so that the mosquito population does not increase so rapidly. What is the number of mosquitos that can be supported in the restricted environment if the population only increases from 200 million to 225 million from this year to next year?

LESSON 44 – COORDINATE GEOMETRY
GRAPHS OF CIRCLES

LEVEL 3

1. In the standard (x, y) coordinate plane, let C be the center and let r be the radius of the circle with equation $(x - 3)^2 + (y + 5)^2 = 7$. Which of the following gives the correct values for C and r ?

    A) $C = (3, -5); r = \sqrt{7}$
    B) $C = (3, -5); r = 7$
    C) $C = (-3, 5); r = \sqrt{7}$
    D) $C = (-3, 5); r = 7$

LEVEL 5

2. In the standard (x, y) coordinate plane, let C be the center and r the radius of the circle with equation $x^2 - 8x + y^2 + 10y + 15 = 0$. Which of the following gives the correct values for C and r ?

    A) $C = (4, 5); r = \sqrt{15}$
    B) $C = (4, -5); r = \sqrt{26}$
    C) $C = (-4, 5); r = 15$
    D) $C = (-5, -4); r = 26$

LEVEL 2

3. Which of the following is an equation of the circle in the xy-plane that has center $(0,0)$ and radius 3 ?

    A) $x^2 + y^2 = 3$
    B) $x^2 + y^2 = 6$
    C) $x^2 + y^2 = 9$
    D) $x^2 + y^2 = 27$

LEVEL 3

$$(x + 3)^2 + (y - 1)^2 = 25$$

4. The graph of the equation above in the xy-plane is a circle. Point A with coordinates $(-3, 6)$ is on the circle. Given that $\overline{AB}$ is a diameter of the circle, what are the coordinates of point B ?

    A) $(-3, -4)$
    B) $(1, 2)$
    C) $(1, -3)$
    D) $(1, -8)$

5. In the xy-plane, which of the following is an equation of a circle with center $(5, 0)$ and a radius with endpoint $(3, \frac{1}{2})$?

    A) $(x + 5)^2 + y^2 = \frac{17}{4}$
    B) $(x - 5)^2 + y^2 = \frac{17}{4}$
    C) $(x + 5)^2 + y^2 = \frac{\sqrt{17}}{2}$
    D) $(x - 5)^2 + y^2 = \frac{\sqrt{17}}{2}$

LEVEL 4

6. A circle in the xy-plane has equation $(x-2)^2 + (y+4)^2 = 36$. Which of the following points does NOT lie in the interior of the circle?

   A) $(2,-4)$
   B) $(1,-9)$
   C) $(-2,1)$
   D) $(0,0)$

9. Which of the following equations describes a circle with radius 6 whose graph in the xy-plane passes through the origin?

   A) $\left(x-3\sqrt{2}\right)^2 + \left(x+3\sqrt{2}\right)^2 = 36$
   B) $(x-6)^2 + (y-6)^2 = 36$
   C) $(x+3)^2 + (y-3)^2 = 36$
   D) $(x-3)^2 + (y+3)^2 = 6$

LEVEL 5

$$x^2 + 14x + y^2 - 10y = -65$$

7. The equation above defines a circle in the xy-plane. What are the coordinates of the center of the circle?

   A) $(14,-10)$
   B) $(7,-5)$
   C) $(-7,5)$
   D) $(-14,10)$

$$x^2 + y^2 - 4x + 6y = -9$$

10. The equation of a circle in the xy-plane is shown above. What is the radius of the circle?

8. In the xy-plane, the graph of $3x^2 - 12x + 3y^2 + 30y + 71 = 0$ is a circle. What is the radius of the circle?

   A) $\frac{4\sqrt{3}}{3}$
   B) 2.31
   C) $\sqrt{23}$
   D) 23

123

LESSON 45 – HEART OF ALGEBRA
ADDITIONAL PRACTICE 3

LEVEL 1

$$a - \frac{1}{3}b + \frac{1}{6}c = 7$$

1. If $a = 1$ and $b = 3$ in the equation above, what is the value of c ?

LEVEL 2

2. A line in the xy-plane passes through the origin and has a slope of $\frac{1}{5}$. Which of the following points lies on the line?

    A) $(10, 2)$
    B) $(5, 5)$
    C) $(1, 5)$
    D) $(0, 5)$

$$C = 49.99 + 0.25t$$

3. The equation above models the total cost C, in dollars, to purchase a prepaid cell phone and send t texts. The total cost consists of a flat fee to buy the phone plus a charge for each text. When the equation is graphed in the xy-plane, what does the y-intercept of the graph represent in the model?

    A) A charge per text of $0.25
    B) A charge per text of $49.99
    C) A $0.25 fee to purchase the phone
    D) A $49.99 fee to purchase the phone

LEVEL 3

$$y = 3x + 5$$
$$x + 3y = 11$$

4. The system of equations above consists of two equations, and the graph of each equation in the xy-plane is a line. Which of the following statements is true about these two lines?

    A) The lines are the same.
    B) The lines are parallel, but distinct.
    C) The lines are perpendicular.
    D) The lines have the same y-intercept.

5. Tickets for a concert cost $4.50 for children and $12.00 for adults. 4460 concert tickets were sold for a total cost of $29,220. Solving which of the following systems of equations yields the number of children, c, and number of adults, a, that purchased concert tickets?

A) $c + a = 4460$
      $4.50c + 12a = 58,440$

B) $c + a = 4460$
      $4.50c + 12a = 29,220$

C) $c + a = 4460$
      $4.50c + 12a = 14,610$

D) $c + a = 29,220$
      $4.50c + 12a = 4460$

6. If $45 - 6x$ is 8 less than 13, what is the value of $4x$?

$$3(x - 2) = y$$
$$\frac{y}{x} = 5$$

7. If (x, y) is the solution to the system of equations above, what is the value of xy ?

LEVEL 4

8. Jonathon purchases a car worth $28,800. The car depreciates at a constant rate for 16 years, after which the car is worth $2200. How much is the car worth 6 years after Jonathon makes the purchase?

A) $15,500
B) $18,825
C) $22,150
D) $25,475

9. Line k is the graph of the equation
    $y = -\frac{1}{3}x + 1$, and line m intersects line k at
    the point $(-1, \frac{4}{3})$. Which of the following
    could be an equation of line m ?

    A) $y = 3x - 5$
    B) $y + 3x = 7$
    C) $x = 7 - 6y$
    D) $2y = x + 3$

10. A retailer ships phones and tablets. Each
    phone weighs 2 pounds, and each tablet
    weighs 7 pounds. A shipment of 83 units
    weighing a total of 301 pounds is sent out to a
    university. How many phones are in the
    shipment?

11. In the xy-plane, the equations $10x - 6y = k$
    and $5x - 3y = 7$ represent the same line for
    some constant k. What is the value of k ?

LEVEL 5

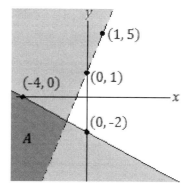

12. The shaded region labeled A in the xy-plane
    above is the solution to a system of
    inequalities. Which of the following ordered
    pairs satisfies the system of inequalities?

    A) $(0, 1)$
    B) $(-2, -7)$
    C) $(-3, -4)$
    D) $(-5, 1)$

LESSON 46 – PASSPORT TO ADVANCED MATH
ADDITIONAL PRACTICE 3

LEVEL 1

1. For the function $f(x) = 3x^2 - 2x + 1$, what is the value of $f(-7)$?

LEVEL 2

$$5x^2 - 6x - 4$$
$$8x^2 - 2x + 11$$

2. If the sum of the two polynomials given above is written in the form $ax^2 + bx + c$, then $a + b + c =$

$$|7 - x| = 3$$

3. The value of one solution to the above equation is 4. What is the value of the other solution?

LEVEL 3

x	$p(x)$
-5	2
-2	-3
1	1
5	0

4. The function p is defined by a polynomial. Some values of x and $p(x)$ are shown in the table above. Which of the following must be a factor of $p(x)$?

A) $x - 5$
B) $x - 2$
C) $x - 1$
D) $x + 5$

5. What are the solutions to the equation $7x^2 - 567 = 0$?

A) $-\sqrt{567}$ and $\sqrt{567}$
B) $-\dfrac{\sqrt{567}}{5}$ and $\dfrac{\sqrt{567}}{7}$
C) -81 and 81
D) -9 and 9

LEVEL 4

6. In the xy-plane, the graph of the function f has x-intercepts at $-5, -3, 0, 1,$ and 2. Which of the following could define f ?

    A) $x(x-5)(x-3)(x+1)(x+2)$
    B) $x(x-1)(x-2)(x-3)(x-5)$
    C) $x^2(x+5)(x+3)(x+1)^2(x+2)$
    D) $x(x-1)^2(x-2)(x+3)^3(x+5)$

$$abc + bcd = ab + ad$$

7. In the equation above, $a \neq bc$. Which of the following is equivalent to d ?

    A) 1

    B) $\frac{1-c}{c}$

    C) $-1 + \frac{1}{c}$

    D) $\frac{ab(1-c)}{bc-a}$

8. Which of the following is equivalent to $\frac{(x^{10}+x^9+x^8)(y^5+y^4)}{y^4(x^2+x+1)}$?

    A) $x^8 y$
    B) $x^8(y+1)$
    C) $x^{24}y^5$
    D) $(x^8 + x^7 + x^6)(y+1)$

LEVEL 5

9. If $x-4$ is a factor of $ax^2 - a^2x - 12$, where a is a positive constant, what are the possible values of a ?

    A) 1 only
    B) 3 only
    C) 1 and 3 only
    D) $1, 3,$ and 4

10. The function g is defined by the equation $g(x) = 3^x + 2$. Which of the following could be the graph of $y = g(-x)$ in the xy-plane?

A)

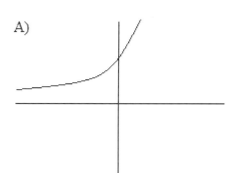

B)

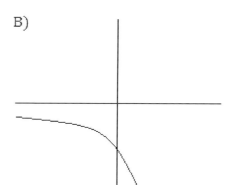

C)

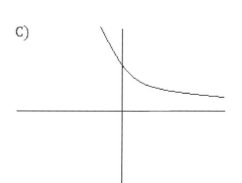

D)

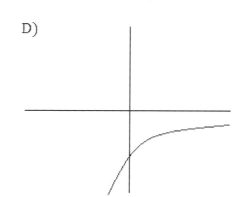

$$3x^2 + 2y^2 = 550$$
$$2x + 12y = 0$$

11. If (x, y) is a solution to the system of equations above, what is the value of y^2 ?

$$y = p(x - 4)(x + 2)$$

12. In the quadratic equation above, p is a nonzero constant. The graph of the equation in the xy-plane is a parabola with vertex (h, k). What is the value of $h - \dfrac{k}{p}$?

LESSON 47 – PROBLEM SOLVING
ADDITIONAL PRACTICE 3

LEVEL 1

1. * An air pump is used to fill at least 60 tires per hour and at most 85 tires per hour. What is a possible amount of time, in hours, that it could have taken to fill 427 tires?

LEVEL 2

2. A tree is growing at a rate of approximately 1.6 feet every six months. According to this estimate, how long will it take, in <u>years</u>, for the tree's height to increase by 8 feet?

LEVEL 3

Questions 3 - 4 refer to the following information.

	Salary Range				
	Less than $80,000	$80,000 −$199,999	$200,000 −$460,000	Greater than $460,000	Total
Male	5	82	57	15	159
Female	3	76	74	18	171
Total	8	158	131	33	330

A group of lawyers responded to a survey that asked what their annual salary was. The survey data were broken down as shown in the table above.

3. *According to the table, which of the following categories accounts for approximately 17 percent of all the survey respondents?

   A) Females making less than $80,000
   B) Females making between $80,000 and $199,000
   C) Females making greater than $460,000
   D) Males making between $200,000 and $460,000

4. * If a lawyer is selected at random, which of the following is the probability that this lawyer will be a male making between $80,000 and $199,999 to the nearest tenth?

   A) 0.2
   B) 0.3
   C) 0.4
   D) 0.5

Questions 5 – 6 refer to the following information.

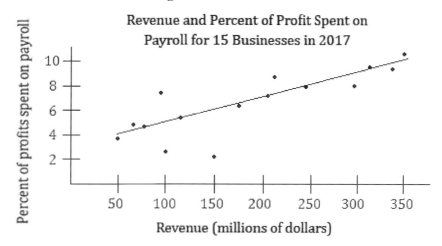

The scatterplot above shows data for fifteen businesses along with the line of best fit.

5. For the business with the lowest percent of profit spent on payroll, which of the following is closest to the difference between the actual percent and the percent predicted by the line of best fit?

    A) 0.5%
    B) 2%
    C) 4%
    D) 8%

6. According to the line of best fit, which of the following is closest to the predicted increase in the percent of profits spent on payroll, for each million dollar increase in revenue?

    A) 0.01
    B) 0.02
    C) 1
    D) 2

131

LEVEL 4

Percent of Students at Six Universities
Who Plan to Apply to a PhD Program

University	Percent of students
University 1	37.2%
University 2	24.6%
University 3	11.1%
University 4	15.6%
University 5	33.4%
University 6	28.6%

7. Students from 30 universities were asked if they planned to apply to a PhD program. The results from 6 of the universities are shown in the table above. The median percent of students planning to apply to a PhD program for all 30 universities was 23.9%. What is the positive difference between the median percent of students planning to apply to a PhD program for all 30 universities and the median percent of students planning to apply to a PhD program for the 6 universities shown in the table?

A) 0.7%
B) 2.7%
C) 4.7%
D) 10.55%

8. For a school project, a student questioned 300 people at random from a group of cat owners. The 300 people were asked if they liked dogs. Of those questioned, 98% said they liked dogs. Which of the following inferences can appropriately be drawn from this result?

A) At least 98% of people who have pets like dogs.
B) At least 98% of people who like cats also like dogs.
C) Most people who do not have cats dislike dogs.
D) Most people who have cats like dogs.

9. A radioactive substance decays at an annual rate of 11 percent. If the initial amount of the substance is 416 grams, which of the following functions h models the remaining amount of the substance, in grams, t years later?

A) $h(t) = 0.89(416)^t$
B) $h(t) = 0.92(416)^t$
C) $h(t) = 416(0.11)^t$
D) $h(t) = 416(0.89)^t$

132

LEVEL 5

Year	Paperbacks sold
2012	1349
2013	4370

10. * The publisher *Get 800* reported paperback book sales as shown in the table above. The percent increase in sales from 2012 to 2013 was approximately triple the percent increase in sales from 2013 to 2014. Which of the following most closely estimates the number of paperback books sold by *Get 800* in 2014?

A) 6880
B) 7100
C) 7420
D) 7630

$$E = 12(1.01)^t$$

11. The equation above models the number of employees, E, working at a company t years from when the company began hiring. Of the following, which equation most closely models the number of employees at the company m months after the company began hiring?

A) $E = 12(1.01)^{12m}$
B) $E = 12(1.01)^{\frac{m}{12}}$
C) $E = 12(1.003)^m$
D) $E = 12(1.0008)^{12m}$

12. How many quarts of a 40% saline solution must be added to 5 quarts of a 25% saline solution to arrive at a 30% saline solution?

LESSON 48 – GEOMETRY AND COMPLEX NUMBERS
ADDITIONAL PRACTICE 3

LEVEL 1

1. What is the sum of the complex numbers $1 + 2i$ and $3 + 4i$, where $i = \sqrt{-1}$?

 A) 10
 B) $10i$
 C) $3 + 8i$
 D) $4 + 6i$

2. A square has an area of 49 square inches. Which of the following is equal to the perimeter of the square, in inches?

 A) 28
 B) 21
 C) 14
 D) 7

LEVEL 2

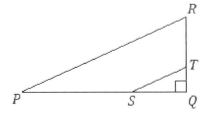

3. In the figure above, $\overline{ST} \parallel \overline{PR}$, $PQ = 8$, and $PR = 10$. What is the ratio of the length of segment SQ to the length of segment ST ?

 A) $1:3$
 B) $2:3$
 C) $2:5$
 D) $4:5$

LEVEL 3

4. A circle with radius $\sqrt{3}$ and center at $(2, -8)$ is graphed in the xy-plane. Which of the following could be an equation of the circle?

 A) $(x + 2)^2 + (y - 8)^2 = \sqrt{3}$
 B) $(x + 2)^2 - (y - 8)^2 = \sqrt{3}$
 C) $(x - 2)^2 + (y + 8)^2 = 3$
 D) $(x - 2)^2 + (y + 8)^2 = 9$

5. In right triangle ABC, $m\angle B = 90°$ and $\sin C = \frac{4}{7}$. What is $\cos A$?

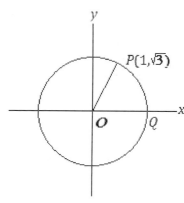

7. In the xy-plane above, O is the center of the circle, and the measure of $\angle POQ$ is $\frac{3\pi}{2a}$ radians. What is the value of a ?

LEVEL 4

6. An ice cube with a side of length 2 centimeters has a density of approximately 0.92 grams per cubic centimeter. Given that density is defined as mass per unit volume, what is the mass of the ice cube, to the nearest tenth of a gram?

   A) 0.7
   B) 5.5
   C) 7.4
   D) 55

$$\frac{7 - i}{6 - 2i}$$

8. If the expression above is written in the form $a + bi$, where a and b are real numbers, and $i = \sqrt{-1}$, what is the value of b ?

LEVEL 5

9. * In right triangle ABC, $m\angle B = 30°$ and hypotenuse BC has length 10. What is the perimeter of the triangle to the nearest tenth?

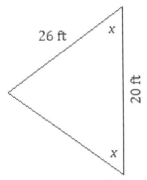

26 ft

x

20 ft

x

Note: Figure not drawn to scale.

10. * A homeowner drew a sketch of their triangle-shaped garden as shown above. Although the sketch was not drawn accurately to scale, the triangle was labeled with the proper dimensions. What is the value of $\tan x$?

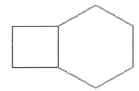

11. The figure above shows a regular hexagon and a square sharing a common side. If the area of the hexagon is $54\sqrt{3}$ square centimeters, what is the perimeter, in square centimeters, of the square?

$$x^2 + y^2 - x + 3y - 5 = 0$$

12. * The equation of a circle in the xy-plane is shown above. What is the <u>diameter</u> of the circle, to the nearest tenth?

PROBLEMS BY LEVEL AND TOPIC
PROBLEM SET A

Full solutions to these problems are available for free download here:

www.SATPrepGet800.com/UniSATxWB

LEVEL 1: HEART OF ALGEBRA

1. If $5 - 11x = 11x + 5$, what is the value of x ?

    A) 0
    B) 1
    C) 2.2
    D) 3

2. A bank charges a fee of \$10 per month to have an account. In addition, there is a charge of \$0.05 per check written. Which of the following represents the total charge, in dollars, to have an account for one month in which n checks have been written?

    A) $0.95n$
    B) $1.05n$
    C) $10.00 + 5n$
    D) $10.00 + 0.05n$

3. In the xy-plane, what is the slope of the line that passes through the points $(0, 0)$ and $(-5, -3)$?

    A) -5
    B) -3
    C) $\frac{3}{5}$
    D) $\frac{5}{3}$

4. Which of the following equations represents a line that is perpendicular to the line with equation $y = -3x - 21$?

    A) $y = -3x + \frac{1}{21}$
    B) $y = 3x + 15$
    C) $y = -\frac{1}{3}x + 7$
    D) $y = \frac{1}{3}x + 1$

137

5. Which of the following is equivalent to $5(x-3) - (x-1) + 4$?

  A) $4x + 8$
  B) $4x$
  C) $4x - 10$
  D) $16x + 4$

$$x + 5 + x + 2x = x + x + x + 3 + 5x$$

6. In the equation above, what is the value of x ?

7. Each cat in an adoption center is given 2 toys and there are 11 additional toys stored in a closet. There are no other toys in the center. If there are at least 23 but no more than 29 toys in the adoption center, what is one possible value for the number of cats in the adoption center?

$$5y = x$$
$$5y = 70 - x$$

8. Based on the system of equations above, what is the value of x ?

LEVEL 1: PASSPORT TO ADVANCED MATH

9. If the expression $3ab + 12$ is equivalent to $3(ab + c)$, where a, b, and c are constants, what is the value of c ?

  A) 1
  B) 2
  C) 4
  D) 6

10. Which of the following is equivalent to $(x^2)^4 x^3$?

  A) x^5
  B) x^6
  C) x^9
  D) x^{11}

11. If $\frac{5x^2}{2y} = \frac{15}{4}$, what is the value of $\frac{x^2}{y}$?

  A) $\frac{2}{3}$
  B) $\frac{3}{4}$
  C) $\frac{3}{2}$
  D) $\frac{75}{8}$

12. If $k^2 - 31 = 17 - 2k^2$, what are all possible values of k ?

    A) 4 only
    B) -4 only
    C) 0 only
    D) 4 and -4 only

$$y = 2x$$
$$x = y^2$$

13. Which of the following ordered pairs is a solution to the system of equations above?

    A) $(-\frac{1}{4}, \frac{1}{2})$
    B) $(-\frac{1}{4}, -\frac{1}{2})$
    C) $(\frac{1}{4}, -\frac{1}{2})$
    D) $(\frac{1}{4}, \frac{1}{2})$

14. For the function $f(x) = 2x^2 - 3x - 1$, what is the value of $f(-2)$?

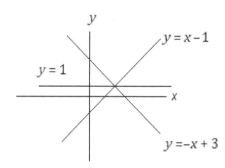

15. Three equations and their graphs in the xy-plane are shown above. How many solutions does the system consisting of those three equations have?

16. The sum of $5x^2 - 1$ and $-2x + 1$ can be written as $ax^2 + bx + c$. What is the value of abc ?

LEVEL 1: PROBLEM SOLVING

17. Joe has decided to walk dogs to earn some extra money. He makes the same amount of money for each dog he walks. If he earns \$360 in a week for which he walks 30 dogs, how much does he earn, in dollars, for each dog he walks?

    A) \$2
    B) \$4
    C) \$6
    D) \$12

Questions 18 - 20 refer to the following information.

A survey was conducted among a randomly chosen sample of 100 males and 100 females to gather data on family size. The data are shown in the table below.

	Have siblings	Do not have siblings	Total
Men	75	25	100
Women	63	37	100
Total	138	62	200

18. How many of the women surveyed do not have siblings?

   A) 25
   B) 37
   C) 62
   D) 63

19. Which of the following is closest to the percent of those surveyed who have siblings?

   A) 31
   B) 63
   C) 69
   D) 75

20. A man who was surveyed is randomly selected. What is the probability that he has siblings?

   A) $\frac{1}{4}$
   B) $\frac{1}{2}$
   C) $\frac{3}{4}$
   D) 1

21. For which of the following lists of 5 numbers is the average (arithmetic mean) greater than the median?

   A) $4, 4, 5, 6, 6$
   B) $3, 4, 5, 7, 8$
   C) $3, 3, 5, 7, 7$
   D) $3, 4, 5, 6, 7$

22. If y years and 11 months is equal to 551 months, what is the value of y ?

Questions 23 - 24 refer to the following information.

A hose is being used to empty a pool. The graph below gives the number of gallons of water in the pool from the beginning to the end of this process.

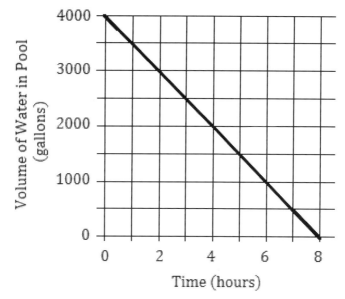

23. According to the graph, how many gallons of water were initially in the pool?

24. According to the graph, how long did it take, in hours, to empty the entire pool?

LEVEL 1: GEOMETRY AND COMPLEX NUMBERS

25. Given that C is the midpoint of line segment $\overline{AB}$, $AB = 3$, $AC = x$, and $CB = 2y$, what is the value of y ?

   A) 0.5
   B) 0.75
   C) 1.5
   D) 1.75

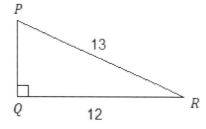

26. Given right triangle ΔPQR above, what is the length of $\overline{PQ}$?

   A) $\sqrt{2}$
   B) $\sqrt{5}$
   C) 5
   D) 7

141

27. A container in the shape of a right circular cylinder has a height of 3 inches and a base radius of 4 inches. What is the volume, in cubic inches, of the container?

    A) 12π
    B) 18π
    C) 36π
    D) 48π

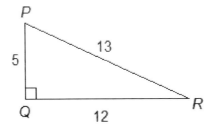

28. In the figure above, which of the following trigonometric expressions has value $\frac{12}{5}$?

    A) $\sin R$
    B) $\cos R$
    C) $\tan R$
    D) $\tan P$

29. The product of the complex numbers i and $1 - 3i$ is written in the form $a + bi$, where a and b are real numbers and $i = \sqrt{-1}$. What is the value of b ?

    A) -3
    B) -1
    C) 1
    D) 3

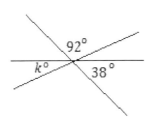

30. In the figure above, three lines intersect at a point. What is the value of k ?

31. What is the radius of a circle whose area is 64π ?

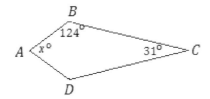

32. In the figure above, $AB = AD$ and $BC = DC$. What is the value of x ?

LEVEL 2: HEART OF ALGEBRA

$$9 + 3c \geq 8 + 3c$$

33. Which of the following best describes the solutions to the inequality above?

   A) $c \leq 1$
   B) $c \geq 1$
   C) All real numbers
   D) No solution

34. In the xy-plane, what is the x-intercept of the line with equation $y = 5x - 1$?

   A) $-\dfrac{1}{5}$
   B) 1
   C) $\dfrac{1}{5}$
   D) 5

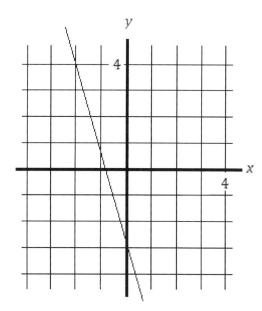

35. Which of the following is an equation of the line that is shown in the xy-plane above?

   A) $y = -\dfrac{2}{7}x - 3$
   B) $y = -\dfrac{7}{2}x - 3$
   C) $y = \dfrac{2}{7}x + 3$
   D) $y = \dfrac{7}{2}x - 3$

Questions 36 - 37 refer to the following information.

A display case containing brass figurines is sitting on a shelf. The weight, in pounds, of the figurines together with the display case is given by the equation $W = 0.7f + 5$, where f is the number of figurines in the display case.

36. What is the best interpretation of the number 5 in the equation?

    A) The weight, in pounds, of the display case when it is empty
    B) The weight, in pounds, of the display case with 7 figurines inside of it
    C) The weight, in pounds, of 1 figurine
    D) The weight, in pounds, of 7 figurines

37. What is the best interpretation of the number 0.7 in the equation?

    A) The weight, in pounds, of the display case when it is empty
    B) The weight, in pounds, of the display case with 5 figurines inside of it
    C) The weight, in pounds, of 1 figurine
    D) The weight, in pounds, of 5 figurines

$$2x \leq 3y + 1$$
$$x - y > 1$$

38. Which of the following ordered pairs (x, y) satisfies the system of inequalities above?

    A) $(0, 0)$
    B) $(0, -2)$
    C) $(2, -1)$
    D) $(6, 4)$

$$3(a + 1) - 7(a + b) = 2a - 7b$$

39. What value of a satisfies the equation above?

$$x - y = 7$$
$$x + y = 9$$

40. If (a, b) is the solution to the system of equations above, what is the value of b ?

LEVEL 2: PASSPORT TO ADVANCED MATH

41. Which of the following is equivalent to $\dfrac{x^4 + x^2}{x^2}$?

    A) x^2
    B) $2x^2$
    C) $x^2 + 1$
    D) $x^2 + 2$

42. If $g(x) = \frac{k}{x}$, where k is a constant, and $g(4) = 3$, then what is x when $g(x) = 6$?

43. Which of the following is equivalent to $(-3x^2y + 2xy^2) - (-3x^2y - 2xy^2)$?

    A) 0
    B) $4xy^2$
    C) $-6x^2y$
    D) $-6x^2y + 4xy^2$

44. Which of the following expressions is equal to 0 for some value of x ?

    A) $|x - 0.5| + 0.1$
    B) $|x + 0.5| + 0.1$
    C) $|0.5 - x| - 0.1$
    D) $|0.5 - x| + 0.1$

45. If $(x - 3)^2 = 36$, and $x < 0$, what is the value of x ?

    A) -33
    B) -9
    C) -3
    D) -2

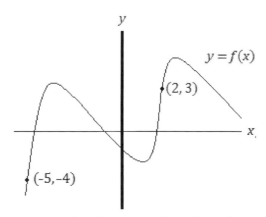

46. The figure above shows the graph of the function f in the xy-plane. What is the value of $f(2) - f(-5)$?

47. If $\sqrt[3]{b^2} = b^k$, what is the value of k ?

$$3(-2x^3 - 3x + 2) - 5(x^3 - x^2 - 3x) = ax^3 + bx^2 + cx + d$$

48. In the equation above, a, b, c, and d are constants. If the equation is true for all values of x, what is the value of b ?

LEVEL 2: PROBLEM SOLVING

49. * A recipe requires 3.5 ounces of red pepper per serving. How many pounds of red pepper are needed to make 60 servings? (1 pound = 16 ounces)

   A) 10.275
   B) 13.125
   C) 100.25
   D) 210

Questions 50 - 51 refer to the following information.

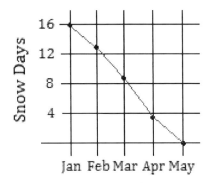

Month

The line graph above shows the average number of days that it snows at least 0.1 inch in Buffalo, NY from January to May.

50. According to the graph, the number of snow days in April is approximately what fraction of the number of snow days in February?

   A) $\frac{3}{13}$
   B) $\frac{11}{25}$
   C) $\frac{3}{5}$
   D) $\frac{13}{16}$

51. According to the graph, approximately what was the least decrease in the number of snow days from one month to the next month?

   A) 2
   B) 3
   C) 4
   D) 6

52. If $y = kx$, where k a constant, and $y = 7$ when $x = 11$, then what is y when $x = 33$?

Questions 53 - 54 refer to the following information.

A survey was conducted among a randomly chosen sample of 150 males and 200 females to gather data on pet ownership. The data are shown in the table below.

	Has pets	Does not have pets	Total
Men	100	50	150
Women	56	144	200
Total	156	194	350

53. According to the table, what percent of the women surveyed do not have pets? (Disregard the percent symbol when gridding your answer.)

54. * According to the table, what is the probability that a randomly selected person with pets is female?

55. To increase the mean of 6 numbers by 5, by how much would the sum of the 6 numbers have to increase?

56. 30 percent of 50 is 10 percent of what number?

LEVEL 2: GEOMETRY AND COMPLEX NUMBERS

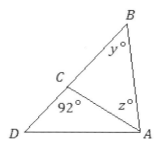

57. In $\triangle ABD$ above, if $z = 26$, what is the value of y ?

A) 26
B) 66
C) 88
D) 92

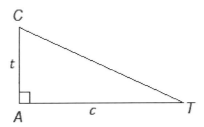

58. Given $\triangle CAT$ above, which of the following is equal to $\frac{t}{c}$?

    A) $\cos C$
    B) $\cos T$
    C) $\tan C$
    D) $\tan T$

59. In a scale drawing of a rectangular garden, the length of the garden is 5 centimeters and the width of the garden is 7 centimeters. The length of the actual garden is L meters. Which of the following functions, P can be used to represent the perimeter, in meters, of the actual garden?

    A) $P = L + \frac{7L}{5}$
    B) $P = 2\left(L + \frac{7L}{5}\right)$
    C) $P = 5L + 7L$
    D) $P = 2(5L + 7L)$

60. The expression $(2 - i^2) + (3i^2 - i)$ can be written as $a + bi$, where $i = \sqrt{-1}$. What is the value of a?

    A) -1
    B) 0
    C) 1
    D) 2

61. The measure of angle P is $\frac{25\pi}{36}$ radians greater than the measure of angle Q. How much greater is the measure of angle P than the measure of angle Q, in degrees? (Disregard the degree symbol when gridding your answer.)

62. The volume of a right circular cylinder is 375π cubic centimeters. If the height is three times the base radius of the cylinder, what is the base <u>diameter</u> of the cylinder, in centimeters?

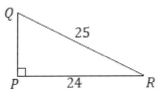

63. Triangle STU (not shown) is similar to triangle PQR, where vertices S, T, and U correspond to vertices P, Q, and R, respectively. If $SU = 12$, what is length of $\overline{ST}$?

64. If $0 \le x \le 90°$ and $\cos x = \frac{5}{13}$, then $\tan x =$

LEVEL 3: HEART OF ALGEBRA

65. A cell phone provider charges customers a onetime setup fee of $40 plus k dollars for each month. If a customer paid $1120 for the first 12 months, including the setup fee, what is the value of k ?

   A) 80
   B) 90
   C) 100
   D) 110

66. Francisco brought $20 with him to school. At lunchtime, Francisco spent x dollars, and during another break, Francisco spent y dollars, leaving him with less than $7. Which of the following inequalities can be used to represent this situation?

   A) $7 - x - y < 20$
   B) $7 - x + y < 20$
   C) $20 - x - y < 7$
   D) $20 - x + y < 7$

$$\frac{1}{3}x - \frac{1}{6}y = 7$$
$$\frac{1}{5}y - \frac{1}{5}x = 8$$

67. Which of the following ordered pairs (x, y) satisfies the system of equations above?

   A) $(-36, -57)$
   B) $(12, 43)$
   C) $(\frac{101}{5}, \frac{307}{5})$
   D) $(82, 122)$

68. The company *Hummus and More* sells hummus in 12-ounce and 16-ounce tubs. During one week, a supermarket sold 423 tubs of hummus, totaling 5820 ounces. Which of the following systems of equations could be used to determine the number of tubs of each size of hummus that was sold at the supermarket, where x is the number of 12-ounce tubs sold and y is the number of 16-ounce tubs sold?

   A) $x + y = 5820$
      $28xy = 423$
   B) $x + y = 423$
      $28xy = 5820$
   C) $x + y = 5820$
      $12x + 16y = 423$
   D) $x + y = 423$
      $12x + 16y = 5820$

149

69. When 9 times the number k is added to 24, the result is 42. What number results when 3 times k is added to 15 ?

70. The graph of the equation $5y - 7x = 11$ in the xy-plane intersects the y-axis at the point $(0, k)$. What is the value of k ?

$$x - y = 2.2$$
$$5x + y = 1.4$$

71. If (x, y) satisfies the system of equations above, what is the value of x ?

$$3k(2 - 5x) = 4 - 10x$$

72. In the equation above, k is a constant. If infinitely many values of x satisfies the equation, what is the value of k ?

LEVEL 3: PASSPORT TO ADVANCED MATH

$$ax^4 + bx^3 + cx^2 + dx + e = 0$$

73. In the equation above, a, b, c, d, and e are constants, and -3, -1, 0, and 4 are roots of the equation. Which of the following is a factor of $ax^4 + bx^3 + cx^2 + dx + e$?

   A) $x - 4$
   B) $x - 3$
   C) $x - 1$
   D) $x + 4$

Questions 74 - 76 refer to the following information.

The entire graph of the function g is shown in the xy-plane below.

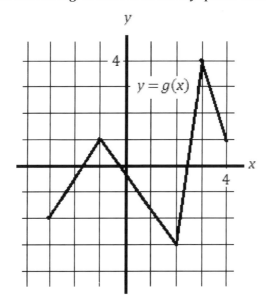

74. For what value of x is the value of $g(x)$ at its minimum?

A) -3
B) -2
C) 2
D) 4

75. What is the minimum value of g ?

A) -3
B) -2
C) 2
D) 4

76. On which of the following intervals is the graph of g increasing then decreasing?

A) $-3 < x < 0$
B) $0 < x < 2$
C) $2 < x < 3$
D) $3 < x < 4$

77. Which of the following is equivalent to $5^{-\frac{1}{2}}$?

A) $-\sqrt{5}$
B) $-\frac{1}{\sqrt{5}}$
C) $\frac{1}{\sqrt{5}}$
D) $\frac{1}{5^2}$

$$X = \frac{3+y}{6} \qquad X = \frac{\sqrt{2y}}{2}$$

78. If the two formulas shown above are used to estimate the same quantity X, which of the following expressions is equivalent to $\sqrt{2y}$?

A) $\frac{3+y}{6}$
B) $\frac{3+y}{3}$
C) $3 + y$
D) $3(3 + y)$

$$\sqrt{3x - 5} = x - 1$$

79. What is the solution set of the equation above?

    A) $\{2\}$
    B) $\{3\}$
    C) $\{2, 3\}$
    D) There are no solutions.

$$h = -3t^2 + 5t$$

80. The equation above expresses the approximate height h, in meters, of a rock t seconds after it is thrown into the air with an initial velocity of 5 meters per second. After how many seconds will the rock hit the ground?

LEVEL 3: PROBLEM SOLVING

81. A patch of ocean containing a single island has a total area of 536 square miles. The area of the water that does not include the island is 412 square miles. The total population of the island is currently 451,000 people. Assuming that the island comprises the total land mass in the given patch of ocean, which of the following is closest to the population density, in people per square mile of land area, of the island?

    A) 840
    B) 1100
    C) 3650
    D) 7000

Questions 82 - 83 refer to the following information.

	Anxiety	No Anxiety	Total
Anxiety Medication	85	165	250
Placebo	115	135	250
Total	200	300	500

The table above shows the results of a controlled experiment that is being used to determine the effectiveness of an anxiety medication. A random sample of 500 adults received either the anxiety medication or a placebo each day during a 1 month time period. The adults reported whether they had anxiety during that time period.

82. According to the table, what proportion of adults who received the anxiety medication reported having anxiety during the 1 month time period?

    A) $\frac{17}{100}$

    B) $\frac{17}{50}$

    C) $\frac{17}{30}$

    D) $\frac{4}{5}$

83. According to the table, what is the probability that a randomly selected person with anxiety was given the placebo?

    A) $\frac{17}{50}$

    B) $\frac{17}{40}$

    C) $\frac{23}{40}$

    D) $\frac{17}{23}$

84. * Of the 400 juniors in Keyton high school, 48% scored higher than 1000 on the PSAT. Keyton high school is part of a school district with 7 high schools and the average size of the junior class for all 7 schools in the district is 400. If the students in Keyton high school are representative of students throughout the district, which of the following best estimates the number of high school juniors in the district who scored higher than 1000 on the PSAT?

    A) 1100
    B) 1350
    C) 1500
    D) 162

85. A survey was given to a random sample of 100 guitar players in Alabama. The results of this survey should be representative of which of the following populations?

    A) All musicians in the United States.
    B) All musicians in Alabama
    C) All guitar players in the United States
    D) All guitar players in Alabama.

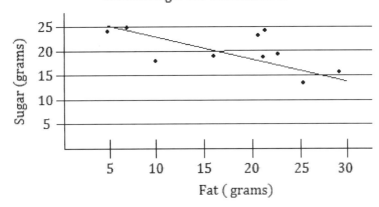

Fat and Sugar for Ten Desserts

86. The scatterplot above shows the number of grams of fat and sugar for ten desserts. The line of best fit has been drawn. According to the line of best fit, which of the following is closest to the predicted decrease in sugar, in grams, for each increase of 1 gram of fat?

   A) 0.1
   B) 0.4
   C) 2.5
   D) 10

Questions 87 - 88 refer to the following information.

A corporate note worth $1200 was purchased at the beginning of the year and since then it has lost 12% of its value each month. The equation $A = 1200(r)^t$ can be used to model the value, A, of the note t months from the beginning of the year.

87. What is the value of r in the expression?

88. * If it is now 6 months since the note was purchased, to the nearest dollar, what is the note worth?

LEVEL 3: GEOMETRY AND COMPLEX NUMBERS

89. In the figure above, $AB = 99$. If $x = \frac{1}{3}y$ and $z = \frac{2}{3}x$, what is the length of line segment $\overline{DB}$?

   A) 11
   B) 22
   C) 33
   D) 35

154

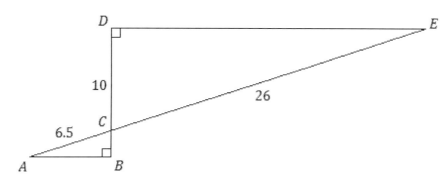

90. In the figure above, what is the length of $\overline{AB}$?

    A) 1.5
    B) 3
    C) 4
    D) 6

91. If k is a positive integer, then i^{4k+3} must be equal to which of the following?

    A) 1
    B) −1
    C) i
    D) $-i$

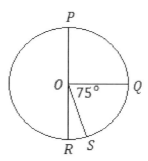

92. In the circle above with center O, $\overline{PR}$ is a diameter, $m\angle QOS = 75°$, and $\overline{OQ}$ and $\overline{OS}$ are radii. If the length of arc $\overset{\frown}{QS}$ is 10π, what is the length of $\overline{PR}$?

93. A sugar wafer in the shape of a right circular cone has a height of 5 inches and contains enough liquid to fill half the volume of the cone. If the volume of liquid in the cone is $\frac{15\pi}{8}$ cubic inches, what is the diameter, in inches, of the base of the cone?

94. In a right triangle, one angle measures $x°$, where $\sin x° = \frac{3}{8}$. What is $\cos((90 - x)°)$?

95. A piece of string is formed into the shape of a regular hexagon, and another piece of string of equal length to the first piece of string is formed into the shape of a regular octagon. If each side of the hexagon is 5 centimeters longer than each side of the octagon, how long, in centimeters, is each piece of string?

96. What is the radius of the circle in the xy-plane that has $(2, 7)$ as its center, and contains the point $(-10, 2)$?

LEVEL 4: HEART OF ALGEBRA

97. A group of friends will be taking a road trip and they need to rent a car. *Discount Car Rentals* charges $50 per day plus $0.50 per mile driven, while *Rent-a-Cheap-Car* charges $80 per day with no additional charges for mileage. The group of friends will need the car for 7 days and they will drive a total of m miles. Which of the following inequalities gives all values of m for which the total charge of renting from *Discount Car Rentals* will be no more than the total charge of renting from *Rent-a-Cheap-Car*?

   A) $m \le 60$
   B) $m \le 210$
   C) $m \le 420$
   D) $m \le 840$

98. To rent a bike, *Guiding Light Bike Rentals* charges $15 for the first hour and $4 for each additional hour. Which of the following gives the cost, $C(x)$, in dollars, of renting a bike for t hours?

   A) $C(t) = 19t$
   B) $C(t) = 15t + 4$
   C) $C(t) = 11t + 4$
   D) $C(t) = 4t + 11$

99. In the xy-plane, line k has a slope of $-\frac{5}{3}$ and passes through the point $(6, -2)$. Which of the following is an equation of line k ?

   A) $y = 6x - \frac{5}{3}$
   B) $y = -\frac{5}{3}x - \frac{2}{3}$
   C) $y = -\frac{5}{3}x + 8$
   D) $y = -\frac{5}{3}x - 8$

$$F = 23{,}200 - 21k$$

100. The equation above estimates the total number of fish in a lake, F, in <u>hundreds</u>, in the kth year after the year 1995. The number 21 in the equation above gives which of the following estimates?

   A) Every 21 years, there are 232 fewer fish.
   B) Every 21 years, there are 23,200 fewer fish.
   C) Every year the total number of fish in the lake decreases by 21.
   D) Every year the total number of fish in the lake decreases by 2,100.

156

101. A carpenter with 400 one-by-four planks of wood wants to make at least 15 tables and 60 chairs. Each table requires 12 planks of wood and each chair requires 3 planks of wood. Which of the following systems of inequalities represents this situation, where t is the number of tables and c is the number of chairs the carpenter can make with the wood planks that he has?

A) $15t + 60c \leq 400$
   $t \geq 15$
   $c \geq 60$

B) $15t + 60c \leq 400$
   $t \geq 12$
   $c \geq 3$

C) $12t + 60c \leq 400$
   $t \geq 15$
   $c \geq 60$

D) $12t + 60c \leq 400$
   $t \geq 12$
   $c \geq 3$

102. Lines k and m have equations $y = 5x + b$ and $y = ax - 5$, respectively. Given that the two lines intersect at the point $(-2, 7)$, what is the value of $b - a$?

103. Dr. Steve creates and sells SAT math problems. He sells "Heart of Algebra" problems for \$15 per problem and he sells "Passport to Advanced Math" problems for \$20 per problem. If an app developer purchased 97 problems from Dr. Steve for a total of \$1780, how many "Heart of Algebra" problems did the developer purchase?

$$5x - 2y = c$$
$$-3x + 1.2y = -9$$

104. In the system of equations above, c is a constant and x and y are variables. If the system has infinitely many solutions (x, y), what is the value of c ?

LEVEL 4: PASSPORT TO ADVANCED MATH

$$f(x) = x^2 - 3x + 2$$
$$g(x) = x^3 - 5x^2 + 6x$$

105. Which of the following expressions is equivalent to $\dfrac{f(x)}{g(x)}$, for $x \neq 0, 2$, and 3 ?

A) $\dfrac{x-1}{x-3}$

B) $\dfrac{x-1}{x-2}$

C) $\dfrac{x-1}{x^2-3x}$

D) $\dfrac{x-1}{x^2-2x}$

106. Which of the following is an example of a function whose graph in the xy-plane can have more than one x-intercept?

   I. A linear function whose rate of change is zero
   II. A quadratic function with no real zeros
   III. A cubic polynomial with at least one real zero

    A) I and II only
    B) I and III only
    C) III only
    D) I, II, and III

107. The expression $\dfrac{a^{\frac{1}{3}}b^{-5}}{a^{-4}b^{\frac{3}{2}}}$, where $a > 5$ and $b > 5$, is equivalent to which of the following?

    A) $\dfrac{\sqrt[3]{a}}{\sqrt{b}}$

    B) $\dfrac{a^2\sqrt[3]{a}}{b^3\sqrt{b}}$

    C) $\dfrac{a^4\sqrt[3]{a}}{b^6\sqrt{b}}$

    D) $\dfrac{a^5}{b^7}$

$$x^2 + 5x + \frac{1}{4}$$

108. Which of the following expressions is equivalent to the expression above?

    A) $\left(x - \dfrac{5}{2}\right)^2 + 6$

    B) $\left(x - \dfrac{5}{2}\right)^2 - 6$

    C) $\left(x + \dfrac{5}{2}\right)^2 + 6$

    D) $\left(x + \dfrac{5}{2}\right)^2 - 6$

109. Which of the following equations has a graph in the xy-plane with two x-intercepts?

    A) $y = x^2 + 4$
    B) $y = -x^2 - 1$
    C) $y = 3(x - 1)^2$
    D) $y = x^2 - x - 2$

110. If $x^4 - y^4 = a$, $x^2 - y^2 = b$, and $x^2 + y^2 = c$, where b and c are nonzero constants, what is the value of $\dfrac{a}{bc}$?

111. If $x > 0$ and $x = \sqrt[3]{\frac{16x}{9}}$, what is the value of x ?

112. If $x > 0$ and $3x^2 - 2x - 5 = 0$, what is the value of x ?

LEVEL 4: PROBLEM SOLVING

Questions 113 - 114 refer to the following information.

$$r = \sqrt{\frac{P}{4\pi I}}$$

Given that the power of the radio signal from a radio antenna is P, the distance from the radio antenna r is related to the intensity of the signal I by the formula above.

113. Which of the following expresses the power of the radio signal in terms of the distance from the radio antenna and the intensity of the signal?

   A) $P = 4\pi I r^2$
   B) $P = \frac{4\pi I}{r^2}$
   C) $P = \frac{r^2}{4\pi I}$
   D) $P = \frac{I}{4\pi r^2}$

114. Emily and Amanda are measuring the intensity of a radio signal coming from the same antenna. Amanda is five times as far from the antenna as Emily. Amanda's measurement is what fraction of Emily's measurement?

   A) $\frac{1}{5}$
   B) $\frac{1}{25}$
   C) $\frac{1}{150}$
   D) $\frac{1}{625}$

Questions 116 - 118 refer to the following information.

Weight Loss

Day	Weight (pounds)
0	250
10	238
20	229
30	218
40	210
50	204
60	195
70	193
80	191
90	190

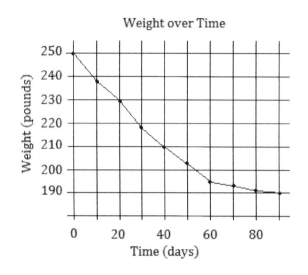

A study was conducted on how a certain nutritional supplement affects weight loss. The table and graph above show the weight w, in pounds, of a single male subject t days after he began taking the supplement.

115. The function w, defined by $w(t) = -mt + b$, where m and b are constants, models the weight, in pounds, of the subject t days after he began taking the supplement during a span of time in which the weight loss of the subject is approximately linear. What does m represent?

   A) The predicated weight, in pounds, of the subject at the beginning of the time span
   B) The predicted weight, in pounds, of the subject at the end of the time span
   C) The predicted amount of weight the subject loses each day
   D) The predicted total increase in weight of the subject, in pounds, during the time span

116.* The rate at which the subject's weight is changing from day 10 through day 40 is nearly constant. On this interval, which of the following equations best models the weight w, in pounds, of the subject t days after the subject began using the supplement?

   A) $w(t) = -0.93t + 247$
   B) $w(t) = -t + 260$
   C) $w(t) = -1.3t + 270$
   D) $w(t) = -2.01t + 247$

117. Over which of the following time periods is the average decay rate of the subject's weight least?

   A) Day 0 to Day 20
   B) Day 20 to Day 40
   C) Day 40 to Day 60
   D) Day 60 to Day 90

160

118. A research study was conducted to determine if a certain supplement is successful in promoting weight loss in women weighing more than 180 pounds. From a large population of women weighing more than 180 pounds, 500 participants were randomly selected. Half of the women were given the supplement, and the other half were given a placebo. The resulting data showed that women who received the actual supplement had lost significantly more weight than those who received the placebo. Based on the design and results of the study, which of the following is the most appropriate conclusion?

    A) The supplement will cause significant weight loss.
    B) The supplement will cause weight loss in all women who take it.
    C) The supplement is likely to cause weight loss in women who weigh more than 180 pounds.
    D) The supplement is better than any other weight loss regimen for women weighing more than 180 pounds.

119. The first family of deer arrived on Staten Island in 2007, and since then the deer population has been doubling every six months. Which of the following statements describes the type of function that best models the relationship between the number of six-month time periods and the population of deer on Staten Island?

    A) Linear growth because the population of deer is increasing by the same amount every six months
    B) Linear growth because the population of deer is increasing by the same percentage every six months
    C) Exponential growth because the population of deer is increasing by the same amount every six months
    D) Exponential growth because the population of deer is increasing by the same percentage every six months

120. An educational workshop is attended by students, teachers, tutors, administrators, and parents. Of those attending, 10% are students, 15% are teachers, 12% are tutors, 23% are administrators, and the remaining 80 people are parents. Assuming that each person in attendance has exactly one of the five roles (for example, no teacher is also an administrator), how many more teachers are in attendance than tutors?

LEVEL 4: GEOMETRY AND COMPLEX NUMBERS

121. The surface area A of a sphere can be expressed in terms of the volume V of the sphere and the diameter d of the sphere by the formula $A = \frac{6V}{d}$. Which of the following expresses the circumference C of the sphere in terms of its surface area and radius?

    A) $C = \frac{4\pi^2 r^3}{A}$
    B) $C = \frac{8\pi^2 r^3}{A}$
    C) $C = \frac{4A}{\pi^2 r^3}$
    D) $C = \frac{8A}{\pi^2 r^3}$

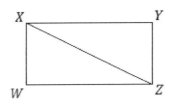

122. In the figure above, $XYZW$ is a rectangle. Which of the following must be true?

    A) $\cos \angle WXZ = \sin \angle YXZ$
    B) $\cos \angle WXZ = \sin \angle XZY$
    C) $\cos \angle WZX = \sin \angle YXZ$
    D) $\cos \angle ZXY = \sin \angle XZW$

123. The height of a trapezoid is doubled and each base of the trapezoid is reduced by 25%. How does the area of the trapezoid change?

    A) The area of the trapezoid does not change.
    B) The area of the trapezoid is doubled.
    C) The area of the trapezoid is increased by 50%.
    D) The area of the trapezoid is reduced by 50%.

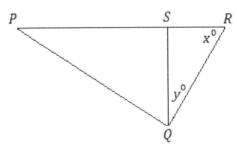

Note: Figure not drawn to scale.

124. In the figure above, if $x = 35$, $PQ \perp QR$, and $PQ = PS$, what is the value of y ?

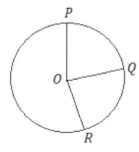

125. In the circle above, radius $\overline{OP}$ has length 2, the length of arc $\overparen{PQ}$ is $\frac{7\pi}{9}$, and $m\angle POQ = m\angle QOR$. What is the measure, in degrees, or $\angle POR$? (Disregard the degree symbol when gridding your answer.)

162

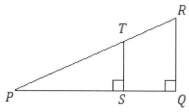

Note: Figure not drawn to scale.

126. In the figure above, $\overline{ST} \parallel \overline{QR}$ and $\overline{QS}$ is one-third the length of $\overline{PS}$. The area of $\triangle PQR$ is 16 and the lengths of $\overline{ST}$ and $\overline{QR}$ are integers. What is one possible length of $\overline{ST}$?

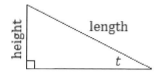

127. A contractor built a ramp such that the sine of angle t, as shown in the figure above, is $\frac{1}{6}$. If the ramp is 10 feet long, what is the height of the ramp, in feet?

128. * If $i = \sqrt{-1}$, what is the quotient when $\frac{5-i^2}{i^2-7}$ is divided by $\frac{i^4-5}{8-i^4}$?

LEVEL 5: HEART OF ALGEBRA

129. The daily cost for a publishing company to produce x books is $C(x) = 4x + 800$. The company sells each book for \$36. Let $P(x) = R(x) - C(x)$, where $R(x)$ is the total income that the company gets for selling x books. The company takes a loss for the day if $P(x) < 0$. Which of the following inequalities gives all possible integer values of x that guarantee that the company will not take a loss on a given day?

    A) $x > 24$
    B) $x < 24$
    C) $x > 144$
    D) $x < 144$

130. A music production company pays a songwriter a royalty of \$0.20 per song downloaded for the first 300 downloads. After the first 300 downloads, the songwriter's royalty increases to \$0.30 per song. Which of the following functions gives the songwriter's total royalty payment, $R(x)$, in dollars, in terms of the number of songs downloaded, where $x > 300$?

    A) $R(x) = 0.20x + 0.30x$
    B) $R(x) = 0.20x + 0.30(x - 300)$
    C) $R(x) = 0.20(300) + 0.30x$
    D) $R(x) = 0.20(300) + 0.30(x - 300)$

131. In the xy-plane, the point with coordinates (a, b) lies on the line with equation $x - y = k$, where k is a constant. The point with coordinates $(3a, 4b)$ lies on the line with equation $2x - 3y = k$. If $b \neq 0$, what is the value of $\frac{a}{b}$?

   A) $\frac{5}{13}$

   B) $\frac{5}{11}$

   C) $\frac{11}{5}$

   D) $\frac{13}{5}$

132. A teacher has c calculators in her classroom, one-third of which are broken. After throwing away the broken calculators, she orders 5 new packs of calculators, each pack containing 3 calculators. After the new calculators are delivered, she now has k calculators. Which of the following equations gives c in terms of k ?

   A) $c = \frac{2k+45}{3}$

   B) $c = \frac{3k-45}{2}$

   C) $c = \frac{k-45}{6}$

   D) $c = \frac{2k}{3} + 30$

133. An ornithologist captures birds, tags them, and then releases them into the wild. Albatrosses are tagged with a plastic tag weighting 0.4 pounds, whereas eagles are tagged with a metal tag weighing 1.1 pounds. The ornithologist's goal last year was to tag 7500 birds. Although he did not meet his goal, he did use up more than 5120 pounds of tags. Which of the following systems of inequalities describes a, the possible number albatrosses that were tagged and e, the possible number of eagles that were tagged?

   A) $a + e < 7500$
      $0.4a + 1.1e < 5120$

   B) $a + e < 7500$
      $0.4a + 1.1e > 5120$

   C) $a + e > 7500$
      $0.4a + 1.1e < 5120$

   D) $a + e > 7500$
      $0.4a + 1.1e > 5120$

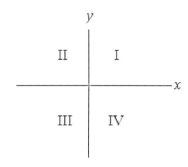

134. If the system of inequalities $x + 2y > 5$ and $3y \leq x$ is graphed in the xy-plane above, which quadrants contain solutions to the system?

    A) I only
    B) II and III only
    C) I and IV only
    D) I, II, III, and IV

$$5k - \frac{1}{3}m = 10$$
$$3k - 2m = 18$$

135. If (k, m) is the unique solution to the system of linear equations above, what is the value of $|m|$?

136. A carpenter spent a total of $5.44 for nails and screws. Each screw cost 2 times as much as each nail, and the carpenter bought 6 times as many nails as screws. How much, in dollars, did the carpenter spend on screws? (Disregard the $ sign when gridding your answer.)

LEVEL 5: PASSPORT TO ADVANCED MATH

137. The expression $\frac{x^2}{5} - 1$ can be written as $\frac{1}{5}(x + a)(x - a)$, where a is a positive real number. What is the value of a ?

    A) 1
    B) $\sqrt{5}$
    C) 5
    D) 25

$$f(x) = (x - a)^2(x - b)^3(x - c)$$

138. In the function $f(x)$ defined above, a, b, and c are constants with $a < 0$, $b < 0$, and $c > 0$. Which of the following could be the graph of f ?

A)
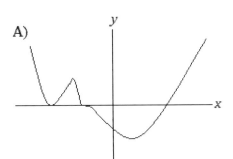

B)
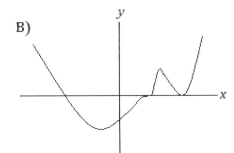

C)
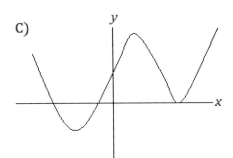

D)
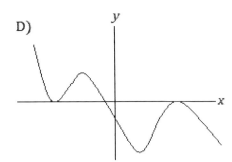

139. Which of the following is equivalent to $\dfrac{3x^2 + 7x - 3}{3x + 1}$?

   A) $x + \dfrac{7}{3}$

   B) $x + \dfrac{7}{3} - \dfrac{3}{x}$

   C) $x + 1 - \dfrac{5}{3x+1}$

   D) $x + 2 - \dfrac{5}{3x+1}$

140. If $\dfrac{7^{k^2}}{7^{m^2}} = 7^{10}$ and $k - m = 5$, what is the value of $k + m$?

   A) 1
   B) 2
   C) 5
   D) 10

141. Two different points on a number line are both 7 units from the point with coordinate -5. The solution to which of the following equations gives the coordinates of both points?

   A) $|x + 5| = 7$
   B) $|x - 5| = 7$
   C) $|x + 7| = 5$
   D) $|x - 7| = 5$

166

142. If $c^{\frac{d}{3}} = 16$ for positive integers c and d, what is a possible value of cd ?

143. If $(2x + a)(dx + b) = 6x^2 + 29x + c$ for all values of x, and $a + b = 13$, what is the value of c ?

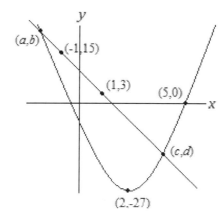

144. The xy-plane above shows the two points of intersection of the graphs of a linear function and a quadratic function. The leftmost point of intersection has coordinates (a, b) and the rightmost point of intersection has coordinates (c, d). If the vertex of the graph of the quadratic function is at $(2, -27)$, what is the value of $b - d$?

LEVEL 5: PROBLEM SOLVING

145. In physics, the force F acting on an object of mass m yields an acceleration a, and this relationship can be expressed by the formula $F = ma$. Furthermore, the amount of work done by this force can be expressed using the formula $W = Fd$, where d is the distance of the object from its starting point. If mass is measured in kilograms (kg), acceleration is measured in meters per second square, (m/s^2), distance is measured in meters (m), force is measured in Newtons (N), and work is measured in Joules (J), which of the following units could be used to represent work?

   I. kg m^2/s^2
  II. m^2/N
 III. N · m

  A) II only
  B) III only
  C) I and III only
  D) I, II and III

167

$$\frac{1}{x^3}, \frac{1}{x^2}, \frac{1}{x}, x^2, x^3$$

146. If $-1 < x < 0$, what is the median of the five numbers in the list above?

   A) $\frac{1}{x^3}$

   B) $\frac{1}{x^2}$

   C) $\frac{1}{x}$

   D) x^3

147. A chef in Japan conducted an experiment to determine if choice in utensils affects how people rate the quality of a meal. The same meal was served to volunteers. Half of the volunteers were given forks and the other half were given chopsticks. The chef concluded that the average rating of the quality of the meal was significantly higher for those that were given chopsticks. Based upon this experiment, which of the following statements is the most accurate?

   A) The choice of utensils was the cause of the difference in the average rating of the quality of the meal, but it is not reasonable to generalize this conclusion to all people from Japan.
   B) The choice of utensils was the cause of the difference in the average rating of the quality of the meal, and this conclusion can be generalized to all people from Japan.
   C) It is not possible to draw any conclusion from this experiment because volunteers were used.
   D) It is not reasonable to conclude that the choice of utensils was the cause in the difference in the average rating of the quality of the meal for these volunteers.

Questions 148 - 150 refer to the following information.

A ball is launched into the air and the height of the ball, in feet, is estimated $\frac{1}{2}$ second after it is launched. The ball is then launched again and this time the height of the ball is estimated 1 second after it is launched. This experiment is repeated 16 times, and on the nth launch, the height of the ball is estimated $\frac{n}{2}$ seconds after it is launched. The results are shown in the scatterplot below and a quadratic model that best fits the data is also shown.

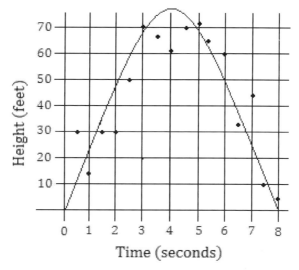

148. Let a be the number of times the model predicts that the height of a launched ball will be exactly 8 feet and let b be the number of times the estimated height of the launched ball was 8 feet. What is the value of $a + b$?

   A) 0
   B) 1
   C) 2
   D) 3

149. For what fraction of the 16 launches is the estimated height an underestimate as compared to the height predicted by the model?

   A) $\frac{9}{16}$
   B) $\frac{1}{2}$
   C) $\frac{7}{16}$
   D) $\frac{3}{8}$

150. For the twelfth launch, which of the following best approximates the percent decrease from the estimated height to the height that the model predicts?

A) 12%

B) $16\frac{2}{3}\%$

C) 20%

D) $24\frac{1}{3}\%$

151. A child starts coloring with a crayon that is 3.5 inches in length. As the child colors, the length of the crayon is decreasing at a constant rate. After 2 minutes, 20% of the crayon has been used. Which of the following equations models the length of crayon, c, still remaining t minutes after the child started coloring?

A) $c = 3.5 - 2t$

B) $c = 3.5 - 0.35t$

C) $c = 3.5(0.2)^{\frac{t}{2}}$

D) $c = 3.5(0.8)^{\frac{t}{2}}$

152. A group of students take a test and the average score is 90. One more student takes the test and receives a score of 81 decreasing the average score of the group to 87. How many students were in the initial group?

LEVEL 5: GEOMETRY AND COMPLEX NUMBERS

153. Samantha, Janice, and Christina are standing so that the distance between Samantha and Janice is 15 feet and the distance between Janice and Christina is 9 feet. Which of the following could be the distance between Samantha and Christina?

I. 6 feet
II. 17 feet
III. 24 feet

A) I only
B) II only
C) I and III only
D) I, II, and III

154. In the circle below with diameter d, chords $\overline{PQ}$ and $\overline{TU}$ are parallel to diameter $\overline{RS}$. If $\overline{PQ}$ and $\overline{TU}$ are each $\frac{3}{4}$ of the length of $\overline{RS}$, what is the distance between chords $\overline{PQ}$ and $\overline{TU}$ in terms of d?

A) $\frac{d\sqrt{7}}{8}$

B) $\frac{d\sqrt{7}}{4}$

C) $\frac{\pi d}{4}$

D) $\frac{3\pi d}{4}$

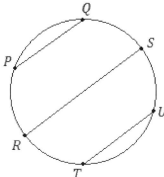

$$SA = s^2 + 2s\sqrt{\left(\frac{s}{2}\right)^2 + h^2}$$

155. The formula above can be used to calculate the total surface area of a pyramid, where h is the height of the pyramid, and s is the length of the square base. What must the expression $s\sqrt{\left(\frac{s}{2}\right)^2 + h^2}$ represent?

A) The area of the square base
B) The area of a triangular face
C) The sum of the areas of two triangular faces
D) The sum of the areas of all four triangular faces

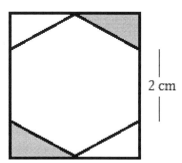

156. The figure above shows a regular hexagon with side length 2 centimeters inscribed in a rectangle. What is the area of the shaded region?

A) $\frac{\sqrt{3}}{2}$

B) $\sqrt{3}$

C) $2\sqrt{3}$

D) 4

171

$$x^2 + y^2 + 8x - 10y - 3 = 0$$

157. The equation above defines a circle in the xy-plane. What are the coordinates of the center of the circle?

   A) $(-4, -5)$
   B) $(-4, 5)$
   C) $(4, -5)$
   D) $(4, 5)$

158. Which of the following is equal to $i^{123} + i^{124} + i^{125} + i^{126}$?

   A) 0
   B) 1
   C) i
   D) $2i$

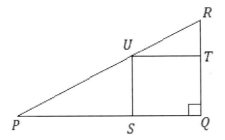

159. In the figure above, ΔPQR is a right triangle, quadrilateral $SUTQ$ is a square, and $PQ = \frac{5}{4}RQ$. The area of the square is what fraction of the area of ΔPQR ?

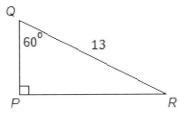

160. In ΔQPR above, point S (not shown) lies on $\overline{QR}$ so that $\overline{PS} \perp \overline{QR}$. What is the value of $\cos(\angle QPS) - \sin(\angle SPR)$?

172

PROBLEMS BY LEVEL AND TOPIC
PROBLEM SET B

Full solutions to these problems are available for free download here:
www.SATPrepGet800.com/UniSATxWB

LEVEL 1: HEART OF ALGEBRA

1. For which of the following values of k will the value of $7k - 15$ be greater than 6 ?

    A) 1
    B) 2
    C) 3
    D) 4

2. To rent an economy car, a car rental agency charges $90 per day plus $0.10 per mile. Which of the following gives the cost, $C(x)$, in dollars, of renting an economy car for one day and driving it for x miles?

    A) $C(x) = 90x$
    B) $C(x) = 90x + 0.1$
    C) $C(x) = 0.1x + 90$
    D) $C(x) = 90 - 0.1x$

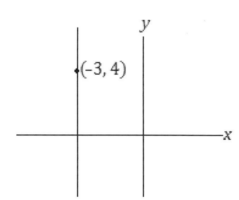

3. The vertical line in the xy-plane shown above passes through the point $(-3, 4)$. Which of the following is an equation for the line?

    A) $x = -3$
    B) $y = -3$
    C) $y = -3x$
    D) $x = -3y$

$$r + g = 25$$

4. The equation above relates the number of red jellybeans, r, and the number of green jellybeans, g, that are in a jar. What does the number 25 represent?

    A) The number of red jellybeans in the jar
    B) The number of green jellybeans in the jar
    C) The total number of jellybeans in the jar
    D) The number of red jellybeans in the jar for each green jellybean in the jar

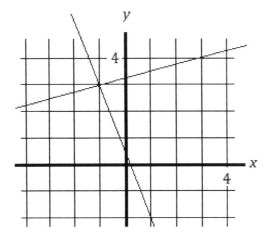

5. The xy-plane above shows the graphs of 2 linear equations. Which of the following ordered pairs (x, y) is the solution to the system defined by these 2 equations?

    A) $(1, 3)$
    B) $(-1, 3)$
    C) $(1, -3)$
    D) $(-1, -3)$

$$y = 2x - 3$$

6. In the equation above, if $y = 17$, what is the value of x ?

7. What value of x satisfies the equation $6(x - 2) = 3(x + 3)$?

8. If $7(2a + b) - 1 = 27$, then $2a + b =$

LEVEL 1: PASSPORT TO ADVANCED MATH

9. Which of the following expressions is equivalent to $3a + 6b + 9c$?

    A) $3(a + 2b + 3c)$
    B) $3(a + 2b + 15c)$
    C) $3(a + 10b + 15c)$
    D) $3(a + 2b) + 3c$

10. Which of the following is equivalent to the sum of $3 - x + x^2$ and $2x - x^2$?

    A) $2x^2 + 3$
    B) $x + 3$
    C) $3x$
    D) $2x^2 - 3x + 3$

11. Which of the following is equivalent to $\left(\frac{x^3}{x^2}\right)^5$?

    A) x^5
    B) x^{10}
    C) x^{20}
    D) x^{25}

12. If $4x^2 - 12x = 40$, what are the possible values for x ?

    A) -2 and 5
    B) -5 and 2
    C) -5 and -8
    D) -5 and -16

x	$p(x)$	$q(x)$	$r(x)$
1	1	2	3
2	2	5	-3
3	5	2	-3
4	-2	4	-2

13. The table above gives some values of the functions p, q, and r. At which value x does $q(x) = p(x) + r(x)$?

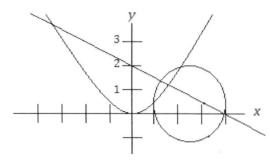

14. The graphs of three equations in two unknowns are shown in the xy-plane above. How many solutions does the system of equations have?

15. If $\frac{20}{x^2+1} = 5$, what is the value of $x^2 + 1$?

16. If $5t^2 - 35 = 13 - 3t^2$, what is the value of $7t^2$?

LEVEL 1: PROBLEM SOLVING

Questions 17 - 19 refer to the following information.

A census was given to determine information about the number of children from households in a small community. 100 families were surveyed and the results are shown in the table below.

Number of Children Per Household

Number of Children	0	1	2	3	More than 3
Households with that number of children	11	21	35	17	16

17. How many households that were part of the census data have exactly 4 children?

    A) 2
    B) 8
    C) 16
    D) Cannot be determined from the given information

18. What percent of the households that were surveyed have at least 3 children?

    A) 8%
    B) 16%
    C) 17%
    D) 33%

19. If a household is chosen at random, what is the probability that the household will have 2 children?

    A) 0.175
    B) 0.35
    C) 0.7
    D) Cannot be determined from the given information

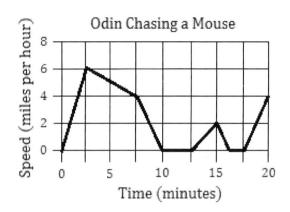

20. Odin the cat chased a mouse for twenty minutes. His time and speed are displayed in the graph above. According to the graph, which of the following is the best estimate for the number of minutes that Odin was not moving during the chase.

    A) 0
    B) 1
    C) 2
    D) 4

21. A box containing 20 ribbons includes 3 red ribbons, 5 blue ribbons, and 12 yellow ribbons. What percent of the ribbons in the box are yellow?

    A) 20%
    B) 40%
    C) 60%
    D) 80%

22. A merchant issued rebates totaling $200 to its customers. Some customers received a $15 rebate and other customers received a $20 rebate. If at least one customer received $15 and at least one customer received $20, what is one possible number of $20 rebates?

23. A company sells advertising for their magazine in blocks of 6 lines of text. If the company places 18 lines of advertising text per page, with 7 pages of advertising per magazine, and 12 issues of the magazine are released each year, what is the total number of six-line advertisements the company can sell in one year?

24. What is the range of the following 9 test grades?

$$89, 66, 75, 91, 56, 92, 76, 71, 76$$

LEVEL 1: GEOMETRY AND COMPLEX NUMBERS

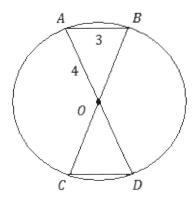

25. In the figure above, if O is the center of the circle, and $\overline{AD}$ and $\overline{BC}$ are diameters, which of the following statements is true?

   A) $OC > 4$
   B) $CD > 3$
   C) $CD = 3$
   D) $OD = 3$

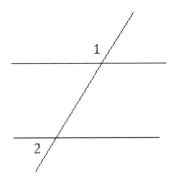

26. The figure above shows two parallel lines cut by a transversal. Which of the following statements regarding angles 1 and 2 is true?

   A) $m\angle 1 = m\angle 2$
   B) $m\angle 1 = 90° - m\angle 2$
   C) $m\angle 1 = 180° - m\angle 2$
   D) $m\angle 1 = 360° - m\angle 2$

27. For $i = \sqrt{-1}$, the sum $(8 - 7i) + (2 + 3i)$ is equal to

   A) $10 - 4i$
   B) $10 + 4i$
   C) $6 - 4i$
   D) $6 + 4i$

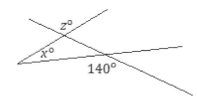

28. In the figure above, $x = 25$. What is the value of z ?

29. If the degree measures of the three angles of a triangle are $k°$, $k°$, and $81°$, what is the value of k?

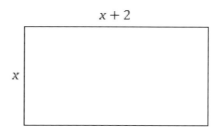

30. If the area of the rectangle above is 15, what is the value of x ?

31. The interior dimensions of a rectangular box are 3 inches by 8 inches by 6 inches. What is the volume, in cubic inches, of the interior of the box?

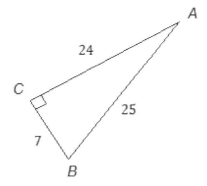

32. In the figure above, what is $\sin A$?

LEVEL 2: HEART OF ALGEBRA

$$19 - \frac{3}{14}x = 7 + \frac{6}{7}x$$

33. What is the value of x in the equation above?

   A) $\frac{14}{5}$
   B) 7
   C) $\frac{56}{5}$
   D) 14

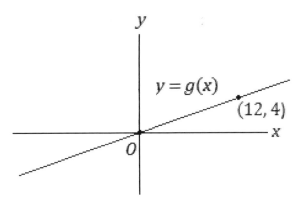

34. In the xy-plane above, a point (not shown) with coordinates (a, b) lies on the graph of the linear function g. If a and b are positive integers, what is the ratio of b to a ?

    A) 3 to 1
    B) 1 to 3
    C) 2 to 1
    D) 1 to 2

35. The graph of which of the following equations is a line that is parallel to the line with equation $y = -2x - 3$?

    A) $2x - y = 1$
    B) $y - 2x = 1$
    C) $4x + 2y = 1$
    D) $2x - 4y = 1$

36. A pipe is used to fill a swimming pool with water. The amount of water in the pool is given by the equation $V = 12t + 200$, where t is the number of minutes since the pipe began filling the pool and V is the volume, in gallons, of water in the pool. In the equation, what are the meanings of the numbers 12 and 200 ?

    A) The number 12 is the rate of increase, in gallons per minute, in the volume of the water in the pool, and the number 200 is the initial number of gallons of water in the pool.

    B) The number 12 is the rate of decrease, in gallons per minute, in the volume of the water in the pool, and the number 200 is the initial number of gallons of water in the pool.

    C) The number 12 is the rate of decrease, in gallons per minute, in the volume of the water in the pool, and the pool holds 200 gallons of water.

    D) The number 12 is the number of minutes it will take to fill the pool, and the pool holds 200 gallons of water.

$$\frac{1}{3}x = 9$$

$$y - \frac{1}{3}x = 2$$

37. The system of equations above has solution (x, y). What is the value of y ?

    A) $\frac{9}{2}$

    B) $\frac{11}{2}$

    C) 7

    D) 11

38. A toy manufacturer uses the function $P(x) = 12x - 1500$ to estimate their profit $P(x)$, in dollars, when they produce x toys. Based on this model, how many toys should the manufacturer produce to realize a profit of $5136 ?

39. * What is the slope of the line passing through the points $(-\frac{1}{2}, -3)$ and $(2, -\frac{1}{3})$?

40. If $7x - 2y = 22$, what is the value of $\frac{3}{11}(7x - 2y)$?

LEVEL 2: PASSPORT TO ADVANCED MATH

$$100x^2 - 64y^2 = (ax + by)(ax - by)$$

41. In the equation above, a and b are constants. Which of the following could be the value of $\frac{b}{a}$?

    A) $\frac{4}{5}$

    B) $\frac{16}{25}$

    C) $\frac{3}{5}$

    D) $\frac{8}{25}$

$$h(x) = kx^3 - 5$$

42. For the function h defined above, k is a constant and $h(2) = 5$. What is the value of $h(-2)$?

    A) -15
    B) 0
    C) 5
    D) 19

$$(2x^2 + x - 5) - (-2x^2 - 2x + 1)$$

43. Which of the following expressions is equivalent to the one above?

    A) $3x - 6$
    B) $-x - 4$
    C) $4x^2 + 3x - 6$
    D) $4x^2 - x - 4$

44. If $2^{3y} = 64$, what is the value of y ?

    A) 3
    B) 2
    C) 1
    D) 0

45. If $c = 3\sqrt{3b}$, what is $3b$ in terms of c ?

    A) $\dfrac{c}{3}$
    B) $\dfrac{c^2}{3}$
    C) $\dfrac{c^2}{9}$
    D) $9c^2$

$$3y = -\frac{x}{2}$$
$$3y^2 - 2y + 1 = x$$

46. Which of the following ordered pairs (x, y) satisfies both of the above equations?

    A) $(17, -2)$
    B) $(-12, 2)$
    C) $(2, 1)$
    D) $(6, -1)$

47. If $x > 0$, what is one possible solution to the equation $x^5(x^4 - 7) = -6x^3$?

$$\sqrt{c - 10} + x^2 = 50 + x$$

48. In the equation above, c is a constant. If $x = 7$, what is the value of c ?

LEVEL 2: PROBLEM SOLVING

49. During a renovation project, a city's main highway was extended from 85 miles to 88 miles. Of the following, which is closest to the increase in the highway's length, in kilometers? (1 mile is approximately 1.6 kilometers)

    A) 4.5
    B) 4.7
    C) 5.1
    D) 5.4

Questions 50 - 52 refer to the following information.

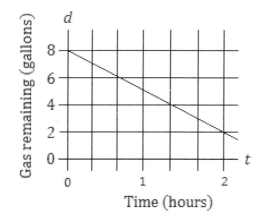

Kenneth is driving from his home to a conference. The graph above displays the amount of gas g, in gallons, remaining in Kenneth's car t minutes after he begins driving.

50. Which of the following represents the relationship between t and g ?

    A) $g = -3t$
    B) $g = -3t + 8$
    C) $g = -\frac{1}{3}t$
    D) $g = -\frac{1}{3}t - 8$

51. What does the g-intercept represent in the graph?

    A) The total amount of gas used during the trip
    B) The total number of hours the trip took
    C) The initial amount of gas in the car's gas tank
    D) The decrease in the amount of gas remaining in the car per hour of driving

52. If Kenneth does not fill his car's gas tank during the trip, when will he run out of gas?

    A) 2 hours after he begins his trip.
    B) 2 and a half hours after he begins his trip
    C) 160 minutes after he begins his trip
    D) 200 minutes after he begins his trip

53. The scatterplot below shows the relationship between the mean monthly heating cost, in dollars, and the mean monthly temperature, in degrees Fahrenheit (°F), in 20 houses in a small town. The line of best fit is also shown.

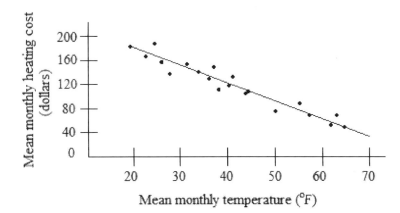

Based on the line of best fit, which of the following is closest to the predicted mean heating cost, in dollars, for a month when the mean temperature is 55°F ?

A) $40
B) $80
C) $120
D) $160

54. * A geologist estimates that a glacier is moving at the rate of 17 feet per year. According to this estimate, how long will it take, in years, for this glacier to move 24.5 yards? (1 yard = 3 feet)

55. A child likes to collect stuffed animals. The ratio of the number of stuffed pigs he has collected to the number of stuffed cows he has collected is 3 to 1. If the child has 6 stuffed pigs, how many stuffed cows does he have?

56. Jeff has taken 6 of 10 equally weighted math tests this semester, and he has an average score of exactly 82 points. How many points does he need to earn on the 7th test to bring his average score up to exactly 83 points?

LEVEL 2: GEOMETRY AND COMPLEX NUMBERS

57. In $\triangle CAT$, $\angle A$ is a right angle. Which of the following is equal to $\tan T$?

A) $\dfrac{CA}{CT}$

B) $\dfrac{CA}{AT}$

C) $\dfrac{CT}{CA}$

D) $\dfrac{CT}{AT}$

58. In the xy-plane, the point $(0,3)$ is the center of a circle that has radius 3. Which of the following is NOT a point on the circle?

    A) $(0,6)$
    B) $(-3,6)$
    C) $(3,3)$
    D) $(-3,3)$

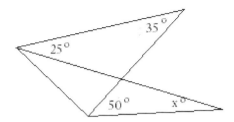

59. In the figure above, what is the value of x ?

60. * The measure of angle X is $12°$ less than the measure of angle Y. To the nearest tenth of a radian, how much less is the measure of angle X than the measure of angle Y ?

61. The volume of a pyramid is $10,000$ cubic feet. If the length, width, and height of the pyramid are in the ratio $2:3:5$, what is the area of the base of the pyramid, in square feet?

62. Each angle of triangle CAT is congruent to one of the angles of triangle DOG. If $DO = 5$, $DG = 6$, $OG = 7$, $CA = 21$, and $\angle T$ has the largest measure of all angles in triangle CAT, what is the perimeter of triangle CAT ?

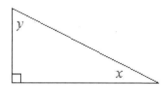

63. In the triangle above, the sine of $y°$ is 0.8. What is the cosine of $x°$?

64. What is the value of the expression $i^3 - i^2 + i$? $(i = \sqrt{-1})$

LEVEL 3: HEART OF ALGEBRA

65. A grocery store sells candy bars individually and in packs of 12. During a certain week, the grocery store sold a total of 315 candy bars, of which 51 were sold individually. Which expression gives the number of packs of candy bars sold during that week?

    A) $\frac{315}{12} + 51$
    B) $\frac{315}{12} - 51$
    C) $\frac{315+51}{12}$
    D) $\frac{315-51}{12}$

66. In the xy-plane, line k has a slope of $\frac{5}{7}$ and passes through the point $(0, 5)$. What is the x-intercept of line k ?

    A) -8
    B) -7
    C) 1
    D) 5

Questions 67 - 70 refer to the following information.

$$C(x) = 2600 + 0.7x$$
$$R(x) = 3x$$
$$P(x) = R(x) - C(x)$$

The manager of a convenience store is submitting a report to the store's owner, estimating the monthly costs, C, monthly revenue, R, and monthly profit, P, in dollars. The functions above express each of these three quantities in terms of the number of customers, x, that make purchases in a given month. The monthly costs, C, consist of fixed costs for rent, utilities, and payroll, and a variable cost for inventory based upon the number of customers in the given month.

67. What is the best interpretation of the number 2600 in the definition of $C(x)$?

    A) The cost for the convenience store to acquire enough customers to break even
    B) The average cost that the convenience store spends per month on expenses
    C) The cost for a month of inventory
    D) The cost for a month of rent, utilities, and payroll

68. What is the best interpretation of the number 3 in the definition of $R(x)$?

    A) On average, each customer at the convenience store buys 3 items.
    B) On average, each customer at the convenience store spends \$3.
    C) On average, it costs the convenience store \$3 to acquire a customer.
    D) On average, each item at the convenience store costs \$3.

69. * The manager estimates that the profit for the month of January will be between \$620 and \$850. Which of the following inequalities gives the best estimate for the number of customers, x, that will make a purchase at the convenience store in January?

    A) $1200 \le x \le 1300$
    B) $1300 \le x \le 1400$
    C) $1400 \le x \le 1500$
    D) $1500 \le x \le 1600$

70. * Assuming that for the month of February the equations given in the manager's report are accurate, what is the least number of customers that need to make a purchase at the store in February in order for the store to at least break even that month?

    A) 1130
    B) 1131
    C) 1132
    D) 1133

$$\frac{1}{3}(3x + 2y) = \frac{7}{3}$$
$$x = 4y$$

71. The system of equations above has solution (x, y). What is the value of y ?

72. At a pet store, each frog is priced at $1 and each salamander is priced at $8. Jeff purchased 14 amphibians at the store for a total price of $42. How many frogs did Jeff purchase?

LEVEL 3: PASSPORT TO ADVANCED MATH

73. The polynomial $z^4 + 6z^3 + 5z^2 - 24z - 36$ can be written as $(z^2 - 4)(z + 3)^2$. What are all the roots of the polynomial?

    A) -3 and 2
    B) -3, 2, and 4
    C) -3, -2, and 2
    D) -2, 2, and 3

74. Which of the following expressions is equivalent to $(9b^2)^{\frac{1}{2}}$?

    A) $9b$
    B) $\sqrt{\frac{9b}{2}}$
    C) $\frac{9}{2}|b|$
    D) $3|b|$

$$3ax^2 + 6bx + 9c + 5 = 17$$

75. Based on the equation above, what is the value of $ax^2 + 2bx + 3c$?

    A) 3
    B) 4
    C) 12
    D) 24

76. The formula $E = \frac{1}{2}mv^2$ gives the kinetic energy of an object with mass m that is moving with speed v. Based on this formula, express m in terms of E and v.

   A) $m = 2Ev^2$

   B) $m = \frac{2E}{v^2}$

   C) $m = 2E\sqrt{v}$

   D) $m = \frac{2E}{\sqrt{v}}$

$$x(2x - 3) = 5$$

77. Which of the following lists all solutions to the quadratic equation above?

   A) $0, \frac{3}{2}$

   B) $0, -\frac{3}{2}$

   C) $-1, \frac{5}{2}$

   D) $-\frac{5}{2}, 1$

78. If the equation $y = (x - 5)(x + 7)$ is graphed in the xy-plane, what is the x-coordinate of the parabola's vertex?

   A) -5

   B) -1

   C) 1

   D) 5

79. If $b = 5a^3 - 2a + 7$, $c = 2a^2 + a + 3$, and $3c - b = da^3 + ea^2 + fa + g$, what is the value of $d + e + f + g$?

$$x^2 + 5x = 14$$

80. In the quadratic equation above, find the positive solution for x.

LEVEL 3: PROBLEM SOLVING

Questions 81 - 82 refer to the following information.

The amount of revenue that a grocery store takes in each month is directly proportional to the number of people that enter the store that month. In January, the grocery store took $2800 in total revenue and 350 people entered the store.

81. * In February, 400 people entered the grocery store. How much revenue did the grocery store make? (Disregard the dollar sign when gridding in your answer.)

82. * The owner of the grocery store donates 12% of the revenue each month to a charity and uses 27% for marketing and other expenses. The rest of the money earned is the retailer's profit. What is the profit in a month where 400 people enter the grocery store? (Disregard the dollar sign when gridding in your answer.)

Questions 83 – 84 refer to the following information.

Fabric	Cost per square foot in US dollars	Cost per square foot in British pounds
Cotton	0.41	0.31
Wool	0.66	0.50
Silk	1.17	0.89

The table above gives the typical cost per square foot of several fabrics in both US dollars and British pounds on November 1, 2017.

83. * If d dollars is equivalent to p pounds on November 1, 2017, which of the following best represents the relationship between d and p ?

A) $p = 0.76d$

B) $p = 1.32d$

C) $pd = 0.76$

D) $pd = 1.32$

84. * If a tapestry using \$41 of material is made entirely from c square feet of cotton, w square feet of wool, and s square feet of silk fabric, which of the following expresses c in terms of w and s ?

A) $c = 100 - \frac{1}{0.41}(0.66w + 1.17s)$

B) $c = 100 - \frac{1}{0.41}(0.66w - 1.17s)$

C) $c = 100 + \frac{1}{0.41}(0.66w + 1.17s)$

D) $c = 100 + \frac{1}{0.41}(0.66w - 1.17s)$

Type of Professor	Favorite activity		Total
	Research	Teaching	
Mathematics	521	326	847
Physics	226	371	597
Total	747	697	1444

85. * On a survey, 847 math professors and 597 physics professors specified whether they preferred teaching or research. The table above summarizes these results. If one of the professors is chosen at random, which of the following is closest to the probability that the chosen professor is a physics professor that prefers teaching?

A) 0.26
B) 0.53
C) 0.62
D) 0.89

86. * A survey was conducted among a randomly chosen sample of 250 single men and 250 single women about whether they owned any guinea pigs or rabbits. The table below displays a summary of the survey results.

	Guinea Pigs Only	Rabbits Only	Both	Neither	Total
Men	92	14	18	126	250
Women	75	42	35	98	250
Total	167	56	53	224	500

What fraction of the people surveyed who said they own both guinea pigs and rabbits are women? Round your answer to the nearest tenth.

87. * A cheetah is running at a speed of 70 miles per hour. What is the cheetah's speed, to the nearest whole number, in meters per minute? (1 mile = 1609.34 meters)

88. The mean score of 10 people playing a video game is 1436 points. If the lowest individual score is removed, the mean score of the remaining 9 people is 1400 points. What is the lowest score?

LEVEL 3: GEOMETRY AND COMPLEX NUMBERS

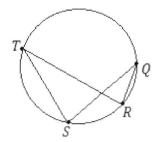

89. In the figure above, angles TSQ and TRQ are inscribed in the circle. Which of the following statements is true?

    A) $m\angle TSQ = m\angle TRQ$
    B) $m\angle TSQ > m\angle TRQ$
    C) $m\angle TSQ < m\angle TRQ$
    D) Not enough information is given to determine a relationship between $\angle TSQ$ and $\angle TRQ$.

Questions 90 - 92 refer to the following information.

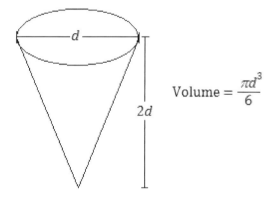

$$\text{Volume} = \frac{\pi d^3}{6}$$

The cone above can hold a maximum volume of 8 fluid ounces (approximately 14.5 cubic inches).

90. How many times can the cone be filled by a jug containing $\frac{1}{2}$ gallon of liquid? (1 gallon = 128 fluid ounces)

    A) 4
    B) 8
    C) 16
    D) 32

91. * Which of the following is closest to the value of d, in inches?

    A) 2
    B) 3
    C) 4
    D) 5

92. A liquid is poured into the cone at a constant rate. Which of the following graphs best illustrates the height of the liquid in the cone as it is being filled?

A)
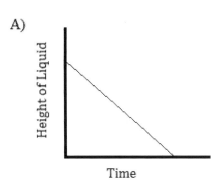

B)
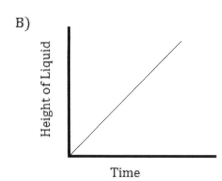

C)
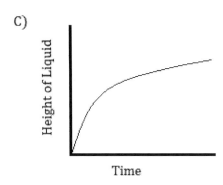

D)
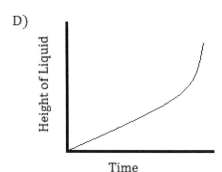

93. A circle with radius 5 and center at $(-3, 7)$ is graphed in the xy-plane. Which of the following could be an equation of the circle?

    A) $(x + 3)^2 - (y - 7)^2 = 5$
    B) $(x + 3)^2 - (y - 7)^2 = 25$
    C) $(x + 3)^2 + (y - 7)^2 = 5$
    D) $(x + 3)^2 + (y - 7)^2 = 25$

Note: Figure not drawn to scale.

94. In the triangle above, x and y are integers. If $39 < x < 40$, what is one possible value of y ?

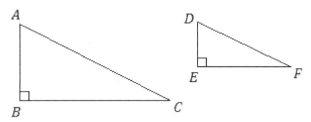

95. In the figure above, the two triangles are similar, with vertices A, B, and C corresponding to vertices D, E, and F, respectively. If $\tan A = 2.36$, what is the value of $\tan D$?

96. The complex number expression $i^2 + i^4 + i^5 + i^8 + i^9$ can be rewritten in the form $a + bi$, where a and b are real numbers, and $i = \sqrt{-1}$. What is the value of $a + b$?

LEVEL 4: HEART OF ALGEBRA

97. A high school has a $1000 budget to buy calculators. Each scientific calculator will cost the school $12.97 and each graphing calculator will cost the school $73.89. Which of the following inequalities represents the possible number of scientific calculators S and graphing calculators G that the school can purchase while staying within their specified budget?

    A) $12.97S + 73.89G > 1000$

    B) $12.97S + 73.89G \le 1000$

    C) $\frac{12.97}{S} + \frac{73.89}{G} > 1000$

    D) $\frac{12.97}{S} + \frac{73.89}{G} \le 1000$

98. In the xy-plane, which of the following does NOT contain any points that are part of the solution set to $5x + 2y > 10$?

    A) The y-axis
    B) The region where x and y are both positive
    C) The region where x and y are both negative
    D) The region where x is negative and y is positive

$$T = 25 + 3c$$

99. The equation above is used to model the number of chirps, c, made by a certain species of cricket in one minute, and the temperature, T, in degrees Fahrenheit. According to this model, what is the meaning of the number 3 in the equation?

    A) If a cricket chirps three more times in one minute, then the temperature, in Fahrenheit, will be one degree higher.

    B) If a cricket chirps three fewer times in one minute, then the temperature, in Fahrenheit, will be one degree higher.

    C) If a cricket chirps one more time in one minute, then the temperature, in Fahrenheit, will be three degrees higher.

    D) If a cricket chirps one fewer time in one minute, then the temperature, in Fahrenheit, will be three degrees higher.

$$5x - 3y = 7$$
$$-30x + by = 9$$

100. In the system of equations above, b is a constant and x and y are variables. If the system has no solutions, what is the value of b ?

    A) -6
    B) 5
    C) 18
    D) There is no such value of b.

101. The graph of a line in the xy-plane crosses the x-axis at the point $(3, 0)$ and the y-axis at the point $(0, -4)$. The line passes through the point $(9, a)$ for what value of a ?

102. A limousine service charges a fixed amount for up to an hour of limousine service plus an amount for each person being transported. A limousine transporting 4 people within an hour costs \$160 and a limousine transporting 7 people within an hour costs \$210. How many people are being transported by the limousine if the charge is \$260, assuming that the limousine service will be used for at most an hour?

$$4x = 5 - 3y$$
$$3y - 2x = 2$$

103. If (x, y) is a solution to the above system of equations, what is the value of $x + y$?

104. While playing a certain game, players obtain blue cards and red cards. At the end of the game, each player's score is obtained by subtracting twice the number of red cards from three times the number of blue cards. A player with a final score of 27 is holding 29 cards at the end of the game. How many blue cards is the player holding?

LEVEL 4: PASSPORT TO ADVANCED MATH

$$5(x - 1)(2x + 3)$$

105. Which of the following expressions is equivalent to the one above?

    A) $30x^2$
    B) $5x^2 - 15$
    C) $10x^2 - 15$
    D) $10x^2 + 5x - 15$

106. If $y = x^{-\frac{2}{3}}$, where $x > 0$, what is x in terms of y ?

    A) $\dfrac{1}{\sqrt{y^3}}$

    B) $\dfrac{1}{\sqrt[3]{y^2}}$

    C) $-\sqrt{y^3}$

    D) $-\sqrt[3]{y^2}$

$$\frac{x}{2} = \frac{3x + 19}{7}$$

107. In the equation above, $3x + 19$ could be equal to which of the following?

    A) -133
    B) -19
    C) 38
    D) 133

108. Which of the following is a value of x for which the expression $-\frac{11}{x^2+3x-10}$ is undefined?

    A) -5
    B) -2
    C) 1
    D) 5

$$x - 3y^2 + 6y + 2 = 0$$

109. The equation above represents a parabola in the xy-plane. Which of the following equivalent forms of the equation displays the x-intercept(s) of the parabola as constants or coefficients?

    A) $x = 3(y - 1)^2 - 5$
    B) $x + 5 = 3(y - 1)^2$
    C) $x = 3y^2 - 6y - 2$
    D) $y = 1 \pm \sqrt{\frac{x+5}{3}}$

110. The function g is defined by $g(x) = (x + 3)^3(x + 5)$. If $g(k - 4.7) = 0$, what is one possible value of k ?

111. In the xy-plane, the graph of $y = (x + 3)^2 - 2$ is the image of the graph of $y = (x + 7)^2 + 1$ after a translation of a units to the right and b units down. What is the value of ab ?

$$2x^2 - x - 3 = 0$$

112. If c is a positive solution to the equation above, what is the value of c ?

LEVEL 4: PROBLEM SOLVING

113. A block is sliding down a ramp that drops 3 centimeters in elevation for every 5 centimeters along the length of the ramp. The top of the ramp, where the back edge of the block is initially placed, is at 60 centimeters elevation, and the block is sliding at 10 centimeters per second down the ramp. What is the elevation of the ramp, in centimeters, at the point where the back of the block passes t seconds after being released?

A) $60 - \frac{3}{5}t$

B) $60 - 3t$

C) $60 - 6t$

D) $60 - 9t$

Questions 114 - 115 refer to the following information.

Boat	Price in dollars	Average monthly fuel cost in dollars
Boat 1	50,000	230
Boat 2	200,000	1010
Boat 3	180,000	906
Boat 4	375,000	1920

During his lifetime, Daniel purchased four different boats. The table above shows the purchase price, in dollars, for the four different boats and the average monthly fuel cost that Daniel paid for each boat, in dollars.

114. The relationship between the average monthly fuel cost f, in dollars, and the purchase price x, in <u>thousands</u> of dollars, can be modeled by a linear function. Which of the following linear functions best represents the relationship?

A) $f(x) = 2.2x + 120$
B) $f(x) = 3.7x + 45$
C) $f(x) = 5.2x - 30$
D) $f(x) = 6.1x - 75$

115. * When Daniel bought Boat 3, he received a 30% discount off the original price, and an additional 10% off the discounted price for paying the full amount at the time of purchase. Which of the following is the best estimate for the original price, in dollars, of Boat 3 ?

A) 185,000
B) 286,000
C) 322,000
D) 450,000

196

116. A phone manufacturer hires a tester to determine the average lifespan of their current phone model. The tester selects 200 phones at random from the phones produced that day and finds that the life of the phone has a mean of 400 days with an associated margin of error of 72 days. Which of the following is the most appropriate conclusion based on these data?

   A) It is plausible that the mean life of all phones ever produced by the manufacturer is between 328 and 472 days.
   B) It is plausible that the mean life of all phones produced by the manufacturer that day is between 328 and 472 days.
   C) All phones ever produced by the manufacturer have a life between 328 and 472 days.
   D) All phones produced by the manufacturer that day have a life between 328 and 472 days.

117. Which scatterplot shows a relationship that is appropriately modeled with the equation $y = ax^b$ where $a > 0$ and $b < 0$?

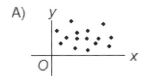 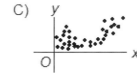 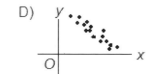

118. The average (arithmetic mean) salary of employees at an advertising firm with P employees, in thousands of dollars, is 53, and the average salary of employees at an advertising firm with Q employees, in thousands of dollars, is 95. When the salaries of both firms are combined, the average salary in thousands of dollars is 83. What is the value of $\frac{P}{Q}$?

119. * Jessica has two cats named Mittens and Fluffy. Last year Mittens weighed 12 pounds, and Fluffy weighed 19 pounds. Fluffy was placed on a diet, and his weight decreased by 20%. Mittens weight has increased by 20%. By what percentage did Mitten's and Fluffy's combined weight decrease, to the nearest tenth of a percent?

	At least 6 feet tall	Less than 6 feet tall
Male		
Female		
Total	15	34

120. * The incomplete table above classifies the number of students by height for the twelfth-grade students at Washington High School. There are twice as many male students that are less than 6 feet tall as there are male students that are at least 6 feet tall, and there are four times as many female students that are less than 6 feet tall as there are female students that are at least 6 feet tall. What is the probability that a randomly selected student that is at least 6 feet tall is female?

LEVEL 4: GEOMETRY AND COMPLEX NUMBERS

121. If n is an integer greater than 35, how many different triangles are there with sides of length 19, 21, and x ?

   A) One
   B) Two
   C) Three
   D) Four

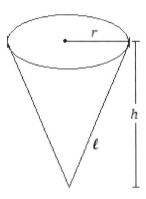

$$SA = \pi r^2 + \pi r \sqrt{r^2 + h^2}$$

122. The formula above can be used to calculate the total surface area of the right circular cone shown, where h is the height of the cone, and r is the radius of the circular base. What must the expression $\sqrt{r^2 + h^2}$ represent?

   A) The circumferences of the circular base
   B) The area of the circular base
   C) The lateral surface area of the cone
   D) The length of line segment ℓ

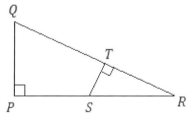

Note: Figure not drawn to scale.

123. In the right triangle PQR above, $SR = 9$, and $QR = 24$. If the length of $\overline{PR}$ is 2 units less than three times the length of $\overline{TR}$, what is the length of $\overline{PR}$?

   A) $\frac{16}{21}$
   B) $\frac{30}{7}$
   C) 6
   D) 16

198

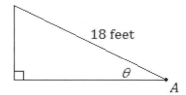

124. * In the figure above a person is standing at point A, and his feet are at a distance of 18 feet from the top of a tree. The angle of elevation, θ, from point A to the top of the tree is 20°. Given that the sine of 70° is approximately 0.94, which of the following is closest to the distance from the person to the base of the tree?

    A) 14 feet
    B) 15 feet
    C) 16 feet
    D) 17 feet

125. Suppose that $0 < k < 90$, $0 < t < 90$, and $\cos k° = \sin t°$. If $k = \frac{1}{3}z - 42$ and $t = \frac{2}{3}z + 12$, what is the value of z ?

126. A rectangle has a perimeter of 22 meters and an area of 28 square meters. What is the shortest of the side lengths, in meters, of the rectangle?

127. In the (x, y) coordinate plane, what is the radius of the circle having the points $(2, -4)$ and $(-4, 4)$ as endpoints of a diameter?

$$\frac{2i - 3}{5i - 1}$$

128. If the expression above is written in the form $a + bi$, where a and b are real numbers, and $i = \sqrt{-1}$, what is the value of a ?

LEVEL 5: HEART OF ALGEBRA

129. Jeff wants to save enough money to purchase and maintain a grand piano. The piano costs $10,000 and maintenance and tuning costs average $40 per month. Jeff has already saved $7,000 and he plans to save an additional $420 per month. Which of the following inequalities can be used to determine the number of months, t, Jeff needs to save in order to have enough money to buy the piano and pay for 12 months of maintenance and tuning?

    A) $10,000 - 40 \cdot 12 \leq 7,000 - 420t$
    B) $10,000 + 40 \cdot 12 \leq 7,000 + 420t$
    C) $10,000 - 40t \leq 7,000 - 320 \cdot 12$
    D) $10,000 + 40t \leq 7,000 + 320 \cdot 12$

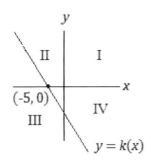

130. The graph of the function $k(x)$ is shown in the xy-plane above. If $h(x) = \frac{1}{3}x + \frac{3}{2}$, in which quadrant does the graph of $y = h(x)$ intersect the graph of $y = k(x)$?

   A) I
   B) II
   C) III
   D) IV

131. An alligator ran at a rate of 8 miles per hour and then swam at a rate of 15 miles per hour. The alligator travelled no less than 5 miles in no more than a half hour. Which of the following systems of inequalities represents the situation, given that r is the number of miles the alligator ran and s is the number of miles the alligator swam?

   A) $r + s \geq 5$
      $8r + 15s \geq 0.5$
   B) $r + s \leq 0.5$
      $8r + 15s \leq 5$
   C) $r + s \geq 5$
      $\frac{r}{8} + \frac{s}{15} \leq 0.5$
   D) $r + s \leq 5$
      $\frac{r}{8} + \frac{s}{15} \geq 0.5$

132. Gary takes a New York City cab 6 miles to work and must pay \$17.50 for the cab ride. After work, Gary takes another New York City cab 10 miles to visit his family and must pay \$27.50. During both of these rides, Gary was charged a "drop fee" (an initial charge when the cab's meter was activated) of d dollars, plus an additional m dollars for each $\frac{1}{5}$ of a mile travelled. What is the value of md ?

Questions 133 - 134 refer to the following information.

The quantity of a product supplied (called the *supply*) and the quantity of the product demanded (called the *demand*) in an economic market are functions of the price of the product. The market is said to be in *equilibrium* when the supply and demand are equal. The price at equilibrium is called the *equilibrium price*, and the quantity at equilibrium is called the *equilibrium demand*. Consider the following supply and demand functions, where p is the price, in dollars, s is the supply function, and d is the demand function.

$$s = \frac{2}{3}p + 15$$

$$d = -\frac{1}{3}p + 99$$

133. What is the equilibrium price? (Disregard the dollar sign when gridding your answer.)

134. What is the equilibrium demand?

$$x + y = \frac{16k}{5}$$

$$\frac{1}{3}x = k$$

135. In the system of equations above, k is a constant such that $0 < k < \frac{1}{5}$. Given that (x, y) is a solution to the system of equations, what is one possible value of y ?

$$-\frac{7}{5}jx - \frac{14}{15} = 3x + k$$

136. In the equation above, j and k are constants. If the equation has infinitely many solutions, what is the value of jk ?

LEVEL 5: PASSPORT TO ADVANCED MATH

137. If $x + y = 2k - 1$, and $x^2 + y^2 = 9 - 4k + 2k^2$, what is xy in terms of k ?

A) $k - 2$
B) $(k - 2)^2$
C) $(k + 2)^2$
D) $k^2 - 4$

$$(x^4 y^5)^{\frac{1}{4}}(x^8 y^5)^{\frac{1}{5}} = x^{\frac{j}{5}} y^{\frac{k}{4}}$$

138. In the equation above, j and k are constants. If the equation is true for all positive real values of x and y, what is the value of $j - k$?

A) 3
B) 4
C) 5
D) 6

201

139. Let x, y, and z be numbers such that $-x < y < z < x$. Which of the following must be true?

    I. $z - y > 0$
   II. $y + z > 0$
  III. $|y| < x$

    A) I only
    B) III only
    C) I and III only
    D) I, II, and III

$$q(x) = (x - 3)(x + 5)$$

140. Which of the following is an equivalent form of the function q above in which the minimum value of q appears as a constant or coefficient?

    A) $q(x) = x^2 - 15$
    B) $q(x) = x^2 + 2x - 15$
    C) $q(x) = (x + 1)^2 - 16$
    D) $q(x) = (x - 1)^2 - 16$

$$x^3 + 2x^2 + 5x + 10 = 0$$

141. The equation above has one real solution, a, and two complex solutions $\pm bi$. What is the value of b^2 ?

$$x^2 + 2x - 1$$
$$2x^2 - x + 3$$

142. The product of the two polynomials shown above can be written in the form $ax^4 + bx^3 + cx^2 + dx + e$. What is the value of $\frac{b}{d}$?

$$\frac{x^2 + 7x - 60}{x - 5}$$

143. The expression above is equivalent to $x + a$, where $x \neq 5$. What is the value of a ?

144. An architect wants to design a bathroom with a rectangular area of 272 square feet. He also wants the width of the bathroom to be 1 foot longer than the length. What will be the width of the bathroom, in feet?

LEVEL 5: PROBLEM SOLVING

Questions 145 - 146 refer to the following information.

743 children from the United States, aged 6 through 11, were tested to see if they were overweight. The data are shown in the table below.

	Overweight	Not overweight	Total
Ages 6-8	31	286	317
Ages 9-11	163	263	426
Total	194	549	743

145. In 2014, the total population of children between 6 and 11 years old, inclusive, in the United States was about 74.3 million. If the test results are used to estimate information about children across the country, which of the following is the best estimate of the total number of children between 9 and 11 years old in the United States who were overweight in 2014 ?

   A) 3,100,000
   B) 16,300,000
   C) 19,400,000
   D) 42,600,000

146. * According to the table, which of the following statements is most likely to be true about children between 6 and 11 years old, inclusive, in the United States?

   A) The probability that a 6-8 year old is overweight is greater than the probability that an overweight child aged 6-11 is less than 9 years old.

   B) The probability that a 6-11 year old is overweight is greater than the probability that a 9-11 year old is not overweight.

   C) The probability that an overweight 6-11 year old is at least 9 years old is greater than the probability that a 6-11 year old is not overweight.

   D) The probability that a 6-8 year old is overweight is greater than the probability that a 9-11 year old is not overweight.

147. A nutritionist wants to determine whether a certain diet improves the performance of members of competitive teams in a certain town. To test the diet, the nutritionist arranges for all the female swim team members from the town to stay on the diet for three months. The nutritionist then compares the performance of these swimmers to swim team members from previous years. Which of the following would NOT improve the quality of the study?

   A) Including members of all the girl's competitive teams from the town in the study
   B) Including women who are not members of competitive teams in the study
   C) Including male swim team members in the study
   D) Randomly assigning half the female swim team members to use the new diet while the other half continues to eat as they would normally

203

Questions 148 -149 refer to the following information.

A diplomat is researching the relationship between the price of a certain export coming from a specific country and the number of adversaries that country has. The diplomat defines an adversary to be a nation that purchases the export, but will not do business with that specific country. 20 countries are chosen at random, and for each of these countries, the diplomat records the number of its adversaries and its price for the export. The results are shown in the scatterplot below and the line of best fit is drawn.

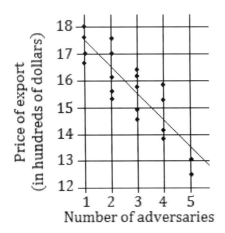

148. The line of best fit passes through the point $(23, -0.9)$. Which of the following can be concluded from this?

    A) A country with 23 adversaries cannot sell the export to other nations.
    B) A country with 23 adversaries cannot decrease its price any further.
    C) A country cannot have more than 22 adversaries.
    D) The line of best fit will not model the price of the export well for a country with many adversaries.

149. A country not shown in the scatterplot sells the export for $1525. If the country's price is more than that predicted by the line of best fit, what is the least number of adversaries the country can have?

    A) 1
    B) 2
    C) 3
    D) 4

150. Which of the following describes an exponential relationship between the pair of variables listed?

    A) Each second s, an airplane's speed r increases at a constant rate of 15 feet per second.
    B) For every 2-centimeter increase in the distance d from the insulated end of a metal rod, the temperature, T, of an object decreases by 3%.
    C) Each day d after a blizzard, the amount of snow on the ground, S, decreases by 2 pounds per cubic foot.
    D) For each increase x by 1 square foot, the price of a New York City apartment increases by $1200.

151. * John, a United States resident, is on vacation in Spain and is trying to decide if he should use his own credit card from the U.S., or to purchase a prepaid credit card for 500 euros in Spain.

The bank that issues John's U.S. credit card converts all purchase prices at the foreign exchange rate for that day, and an additional fee of 6% of the converted cost is applied before the bank posts the charge.

If John decides to purchase the prepaid card, he can use this card spending dollars at the exchange rate for that day with no fee, but he loses any money left unspent on the card.

Suppose that John does decide to buy the prepaid card. What is the least number of the 500 euros John must spend for the prepaid card to have been the cheaper option? Round your answer to the nearest whole number of euros.

152. For 5 numbers in a list of increasing numbers, the average (arithmetic mean), median, and mode are all equal to 11. The range of the list is 7. The second number in the list is less than 11 and 2 more than the least number in the list. What is the greatest number in the list?

LEVEL 5: GEOMETRY AND COMPLEX NUMBERS

153. A square is inscribed in a circle of diameter d. What is the perpendicular distance from the center of the circle to a side of the square, in terms of d ?

   A) $\frac{d}{2}$

   B) $\frac{d\sqrt{2}}{4}$

   C) $\frac{d\sqrt{2}}{2}$

   D) d

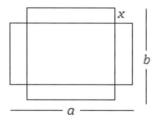

154. A square with sides of length x centimeters has been removed from each corner of a rectangular sheet of metal with length a and width b. The metal is then folded upward to form an open box. Which of the following quantities is equal to $2x(a + b - 4x)$?

   A) The volume of the interior of the closed box
   B) The surface area of the closed box
   C) The area of the five faces of the box
   D) The area of the four lateral faces of the box

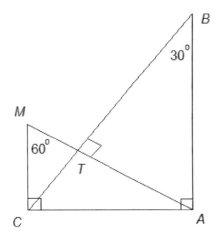

155. For the triangles in the figure above, which of the following ratios of side lengths is equivalent to the ratio of the perimeter of $\triangle CBA$ to the perimeter of $\triangle MAC$?

    A) $AB:CA$
    B) $AB:AM$
    C) $AB:BC$
    D) $AB:CM$

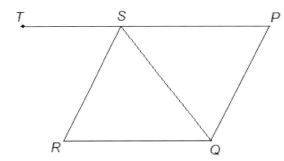

156. In the figure above, $\overline{QS}$ is the shorter diagonal of rhombus $PQRS$ and T is on $\overrightarrow{PS}$. The measure of angle PQS is $x°$. What is the measure of RST, in terms of x ?

    A) $x°$
    B) $2x°$
    C) $(90 - x)°$
    D) $(180 - x)°$

157. The circumference of the base of a right circular cone is 10π and the circumference of a parallel cross section is 8π. If the distance between the base and the cross section is 6, what is the height of the cone?

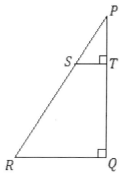

Note: Figure not drawn to scale.

158. In the figure above, $\cos P = \frac{12}{13}$. If $RQ = 10$ and $TQ = 3$, what is the length of $\overline{RS}$?

$$x^2 + y^2 - 3x + 5y - \frac{1}{2} = 0$$

159. The equation above defines a circle in the xy-plane. What is the <u>diameter</u> of the circle?

160. Let $x = 1 + i$, $y = 1 - i$, $z = 2 + 3i$, $w = \frac{x}{y}$, and $u = \frac{w}{z}$. When u is written in the form $a + bi$, what is the value of $13(a + b)$? (Note that $i = \sqrt{-1}$)

 **PROBLEMS BY LEVEL AND TOPIC**
PROBLEM SET C

Full solutions to these problems are available for free download here:
www.SATPrepGet800.com/UniSATxWB

LEVEL 1: HEART OF ALGEBRA

1. If $\frac{10}{9}k = \frac{3}{5}$, what is the value of k ?

   A) $\frac{2}{3}$

   B) $\frac{27}{50}$

   C) $\frac{9}{25}$

   D) $\frac{1}{5}$

2. A veterinarian charges a pet owner \$150 for an office visit, as well as \$50 for each test that needs to be run and \$30 for each medication that needs to be prescribed. Which of the following expressions best models the total cost, in dollars, to bring in a pet that requires t tests and m medications?

   A) $(50 + 30)(t + m)$
   B) $(50 + 30)(t + m) - 150$
   C) $(50 + 150)t + 30m$
   D) $150 + 50t + 30m$

3. Which of the following statements is true regarding the line with equation $y = -5$?

   A) The line is vertical.
   B) The line is horizontal.
   C) The line has a positive slope.
   D) The line has a negative slope.

$$20t + 5c = 240$$

4. Daniel is playing poker with some friends. The equation above can be used to model the number of chips, c, that Daniel still has in his possession t hours after he begins playing. What does it mean that $t = 0, c = 48$ is a solution to this equation?

   A) Daniel is losing 48 chips per hour.
   B) It would take 48 hours for Daniel to have 240 chips.
   C) Daniel can play for 48 hours before losing all his chips.
   D) Daniel begins playing with 48 chips.

$$F = \frac{9}{5}C + 32$$

5. The formula above shows how a temperature C, measured in degrees Celsius, relates to a temperature F, measured in degrees Fahrenheit. What is C in terms of F ?

   A) $C = \frac{5}{9}F + 32$

   B) $C = \frac{5}{9}F - 32$

   C) $C = \frac{5}{9}(F - 32)$

   D) $C = \frac{9}{5}F + 32$

$$x = 3 - y$$
$$5y = 15$$

6. Which of the following ordered pairs (x, y) satisfies the system of equations above?

   A) $(6, 3)$
   B) $(1, 2)$
   C) $(3, 0)$
   D) $(0, 3)$

7. If $3\left(\frac{x-4}{7}\right) = d$ and $d = 15$, what is the value of x ?

8. The function W defined by $W(a) = 1.9a + 2.3$ models the weight of a kitten, in ounces, that is a weeks old for $0 \le a \le 6$. According to this model, what is the weight, in ounces, of a kitten that is 3 weeks old?

LEVEL 1: PASSPORT TO ADVANCED MATH

9. If $f(x) = 2 - 5(x^2 + 1)$, which of the following is equivalent to $f(x)$?

   A) $3 - 5x^2$
   B) $-3 - 5x^2$
   C) $7 - 5x^2$
   D) $1 - 5x^2$

10. Which of the following graphs could not be the graph of a function?

A)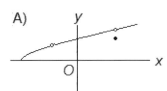

B)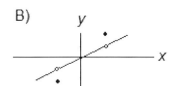

C)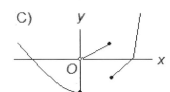

D)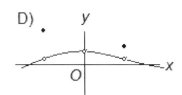

11. For which nonnegative value of k is the expression $\frac{1}{4-k^2}$ undefined?

    A) 0
    B) $\sqrt{2}$
    C) 2
    D) 4

$$y = 2x^2$$
$$x = 2y$$

12. Which value is a y-coordinate of a solution to the system of equations above?

    A) 1
    B) $\frac{1}{2}$
    C) $\frac{1}{4}$
    D) $\frac{1}{8}$

13. If $3a(2b + 5c) = jab + kac$, where $a, b, c, j,$ and k are constants, what is the value of jk ?

14. If $3^{x+1} = 27$, what is the value of x ?

15. If $x^2 = 3yz$, what is the value of $\frac{x^2}{yz}$?

16. If $c > 0$, for what value of c will $\frac{c^2+13}{7} = 11$?

LEVEL 1: PROBLEM SOLVING

17. The ratio of 29 to 5 is equal to the ratio of 203 to what number?

    A) $\frac{1}{35}$
    B) $\frac{5}{7}$
    C) $\frac{7}{5}$
    D) 35

18. A store owner buys and sells watches, always keeping track of how many watches he has available for sale in his store. This data is shown on the graph below.

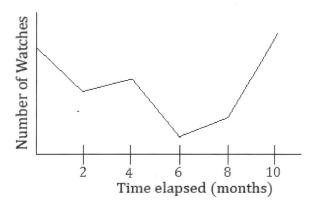

When did the store owner have the least number of watches?

    A) After 2 months
    B) After 4 months
    C) After 6 months
    D) After 8 months

Questions 18 - 21 refer to the following information.

Ten 25-year-old men were asked how many hours per week they exercise and their resting heart rate was taken in beats per minute (BPM). The results are shown as points in the scatterplot below, and the line of best fit is drawn.

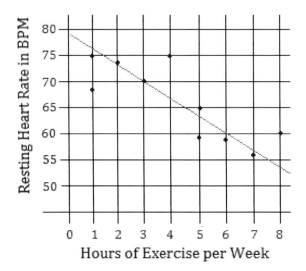

19. How many of the men have a resting heart rate that differs by more than 5 BPM from the resting heart rate predicted by the line of best fit?

   A) None
   B) Two
   C) Three
   D) Four

20. Based on the line of best fit, what is the predicted resting heart rate for someone that exercises three and a half hours per week?

   A) 66 BPM
   B) 68 BPM
   C) 70 BPM
   D) 72 BPM

21. What is the resting heart rate, in BPM, of the man represented by the data point that is farthest from the line of best fit?

   A) 60
   B) 66
   C) 68
   D) 75

22. Which of the following is the best interpretation of the slope of the line of best fit in the context of this problem?

    A) The predicted number of hours that a person must exercise to maintain a resting heart rate of 50 BPM

    B) The predicted resting heart rate of a person that does not exercise

    C) The predicted decrease in resting heart rate, in BPM, for each one hour increase in weekly exercise

    D) The predicted increase in the number of hours of exercise needed to increase the resting heart rate by one BPM

23. The mass of an object is equal to the product of the volume of the object and the density of the object. What is the density of an object, in kilograms per cubic meter, of an object with a mass of 40 kilograms and a volume of 10 cubic meters?

24. Dan, Craig, Phil, and John own a total of 37 paintings. If Dan owns 10 of them, what is the average (arithmetic mean) number of paintings owned by John, Craig, and Phil?

LEVEL 1: GEOMETRY AND COMPLEX NUMBERS

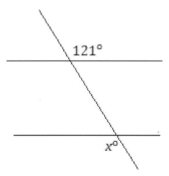

25. The figure above shows two parallel lines cut by a transversal. What is the value of x ?

    A) 31
    B) 59
    C) 121
    D) 239

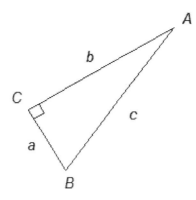

26. The dimensions of the right triangle above are given in meters. What is $\cos A$?

    A) $\dfrac{b}{a}$

    B) $\dfrac{b}{c}$

    C) $\dfrac{a}{b}$

    D) $\dfrac{c}{b}$

27. For $i = \sqrt{-1}$, which of the following is equivalent to $i + 2i^2$?

    A) $2 + i$
    B) $2 - i$
    C) $-2 + i$
    D) $-2 - i$

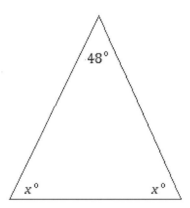

28. In the triangle above, what is the value of x ?

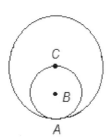

29. In the figure above, A, B, and C lie on the same line. B is the center of the smaller circle, and C is the center of the larger circle. If the radius of the smaller circle is 3, what is the diameter of the larger circle?

30. A pyramid has a rectangular base. The length of the base is 3 feet and the width of the base is 5 feet. If the height of the pyramid is 10 feet, what is the volume of the pyramid, in cubic feet?

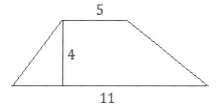

31. What is the area of the trapezoid shown above?

32. For $i = \sqrt{-1}$, when we add the complex numbers $5i$, $6 + i$, and $2 - 2i$, we get the complex number $a + bi$. What is the value of b ?

LEVEL 2: HEART OF ALGEBRA

33. Gina subscribes to a cell phone service that charges a monthly fee of $60.00. The first 500 megabytes of data are free, and the cost is $0.15 for each additional megabyte of data used that month. Which of the following functions gives the cost, in dollars, for a month in which Gina uses x megabytes of data, where $x > 500$?

    A) $60 + 15x$
    B) $0.15x - 15$
    C) $0.15x - 440$
    D) $60 + 0.15x$

34. The line $y = mx + b$, where m and b are constants, is graphed in the xy-plane. If the line contains the point (c, d) where c and d are nonzero, what is b in terms of c and d ?

    A) $d - mc$
    B) $d + mc$
    C) $\frac{d-m}{c}$
    D) $\frac{d-c}{m}$

35. Which of the following is the graph of the equation $y = -\frac{1}{2}x + 3$ in the xy-plane?

A)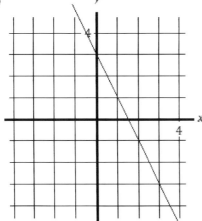

B)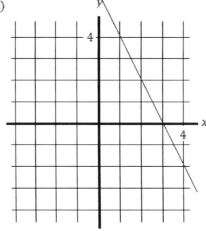

C)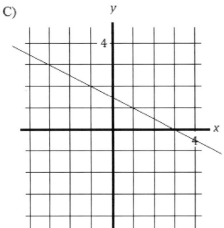

D)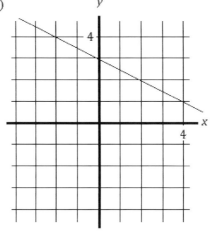

36. The graph of which of the following equations in the xy-plane is a line with slope -5 ?

A) $y = -5x$

B) $y = -\frac{1}{5}x$

C) $y = \frac{1}{5}x$

D) $y = 5x$

37. If $3x = 9y$, what is the value of $\frac{6y}{x}$?

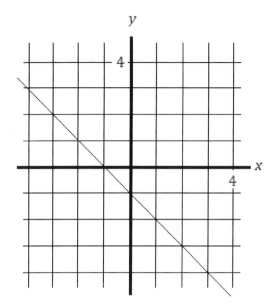

38. A line is shown in the xy-plane above. A second line (not shown) is parallel to the line shown and passes through the points $(1, -5)$ and $(-7, k)$, where k is a constant. What is the value of k ?

39. A florist is currently selling 12 different types of bouquets. The florist plans to introduce 3 new types of bouquets every year for the next 4 years. If an equation in the form $b = mt + k$ is used to represent the number of bouquets, b, that the florist will have available t years from now, what is the value of k ?

$$52k + 34b = C$$

40. * The equation above gives the monthly cost C, in dollars, to take care of k kittens and b bunnies. John has 3 kittens and 5 bunnies, and Jenny has 2 kittens and 3 bunnies. How much greater, in dollars, is John's total cost than Jenny's total cost to take care of their respective pets? (Disregard the dollar sign when gridding your answer.)

LEVEL 2: PASSPORT TO ADVANCED MATH

$$7x^2 + 5x(3 - x) - 4(x - 2)$$

41. Which of the following polynomials is equivalent to the expression above?

A) $7x^2 - 10x - 8$
B) $7x^2 + 10x + 8$
C) $2x^2 + 11x + 8$
D) $2x^2 - 11x - 8$

42. Which of the following is equal to $b^{\frac{2}{3}}$ for all values of b ?

  A) $\sqrt[3]{b^2}$
  B) $\sqrt{b^3}$
  C) $\sqrt{b^{\frac{1}{3}}}$
  D) $\sqrt[3]{b^{\frac{1}{2}}}$

$$\sqrt{2b^2 + 21} - a = 0$$

43. If $a = 5$ in the equation above, which of the following is a possible value of b ?

  A) -2
  B) $-\sqrt{2}$
  C) 0
  D) 3

44. Suppose that $g(x) = 2x^2 - 5$, $g(k) = 45$, and $k > 0$. What is the value of k ?

45. The function f is defined by the equation $f(x) = 2^x - 3x + 1$. The point $(4, b)$ lies on the graph of f. What is the value of b?

46. If $\frac{5c}{d} = \frac{10}{3}$, what is the value of $\frac{d}{c}$?

47. The expression $(x^2 + 3) - (-2x^2 + x - 5)$ can be written in the form $ax^2 + bx + c$. What is the value of $a + b + c$?

48. What is the sum of the solutions to the equation $(x - 6)(x + 1.2) = 0$?

LEVEL 2: PROBLEM SOLVING

49. Each bundle of wires inside a large machine needs to be secured with 5 centimeters of electrical tape. What is the maximum number of these wire bundles that can be secured with 8 meters of electrical tape? (1 meter = 100 centimeters)

  A) 80
  B) 160
  C) 200
  D) 320

Questions 50 - 51 refer to the following information.

The table below shows the distribution of the five types of birds in an aviary.

Types of birds	Percent in aviary
Pelican	15%
Flamingo	8%
Water Thrush	25%
Stork	12%
Heron	40%

50. If a bird is selected at random from the aviary, what is the probability that the bird will NOT be a pelican?

   A) $\frac{3}{20}$

   B) $\frac{1}{4}$

   C) $\frac{2}{5}$

   D) $\frac{17}{20}$

51. If there are 60 more herons than pelicans in the aviary, what is the total number of birds in the aviary?

   A) 120
   B) 200
   C) 240
   D) 400

52. Which scatterplot shows a nonlinear positive association? (Note: A positive association between two variables is one in which higher values of one variable correspond to higher values of the other variable.)

A)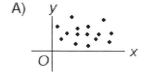

B)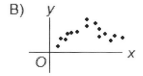

C)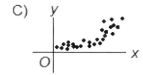

D)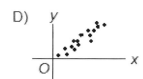

53. In 1980, an ounce of silver was worth $50. How heavy, in pounds, was $12,500 worth of silver in 1980? (16 ounces = 1 pound)

219

54. The weight of a liquid in a container is directly proportional to the volume of the liquid. Suppose that 4 gallons of a certain liquid weighs 5 pounds. What is the weight, in pounds, of 10 gallons of the same liquid?

55. * The *mina*, a Babylonian measure of weight, is approximately equal to 640 grams. It is also equivalent to 60 smaller Babylonian units called *talents*. Based on these relationships, 100 Babylonian talents is equivalent to how many <u>ounces</u>, to the nearest tenth? (28.35 grams = 1 ounce)

56. * What percent of 75 is 32 ? (Disregard the percent symbol when gridding in your answer.)

LEVEL 2: GEOMETRY AND COMPLEX NUMBERS

57. Violet is 5 feet tall and at a certain moment, the straight-line distance from the top of her head to the tip of her shadow is 13 feet. At this point in time, how long is violet's shadow?

    A) 8 feet.
    B) 9 feet
    C) 12 feet
    D) 14 feet

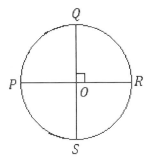

58. In the circle above with center O, $OR = 5$. What is the length of minor arc $\overgroup{RS}$?

    A) $\dfrac{5\pi}{2}$

    B) $\dfrac{5\pi}{4}$

    C) $\dfrac{5\pi}{8}$

    D) $\dfrac{5\pi}{12}$

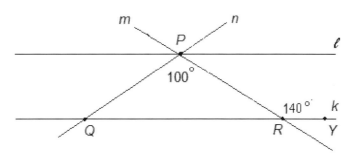

59. In the figure above, line ℓ is parallel to line k. Transversals m and n intersect at point P on ℓ and intersect k at points R and Q, respectively. Point Y is on k, the measure of $\angle PRY$ is 140°, and the measure of $\angle QPR$ is 100°. How many of the angles formed by rays ℓ, k, m, and n have measure 40° ?

    A) 4
    B) 6
    C) 8
    D) 10

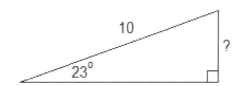

60. As shown above, a 10-foot ramp forms an angle of 23° with the ground, which is horizontal. Which of the following is an expression for the vertical rise, in feet, of the ramp?

    A) $10 \cos 23°$
    B) $10 \sin 23°$
    C) $10 \tan 23°$
    D) $10 \cot 23°$

61. If k is a positive integer, then i^{4k} must be equal to which of the following?

    A) 1
    B) -1
    C) i
    D) $-i$

62. The volume of a right circular cone is 72π cubic inches. If the height of the cone is equal to the base radius of the cone, what is the height of the cone, in inches?

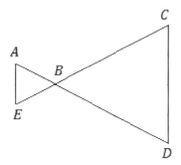

63. In the figure above, $\overline{AE} \parallel \overline{CD}$, $\overline{AB} \cong \overline{BE}$, and $m\angle ABE = 40°$. What is the measure, in degrees, of angle C ? (Disregard the degree sign when gridding in your answer.)

$$(x - 5)^2 + (y + 2)^2 = 9$$

64. The graph of the equation above in the xy-plane is a circle. What is the radius of the circle?

LEVEL 3: HEART OF ALGEBRA

65. During the second voyage of the HMS Beagle, Charles Darwin travelled from Plymouth Sound to Tenerife, stopping at Madeira along the way. The total distance he travelled during this part of his journey was 3275 miles, and the distance from Plymouth Sound to Madeira was 2657 miles more than the distance from Madeira to Tenerife. What was the distance from Madeira to Tenerif, in miles?

A) 309
B) 350
C) 420
D) 515

66. A line is graphed in the xy-plane. If the line has a negative slope and a positive y-intercept, which of the following points cannot lie on the line?

A) $(-1, -1)$
B) $(1, -1)$
C) $(-1, 1)$
D) $(1, 1)$

$$y = \frac{x}{2} - 5$$
$$x + \frac{y}{2} = \frac{5}{2}$$

67. Which of the following ordered pairs (x, y) satisfies the system of equations above?

A) $(1, 3)$
B) $(2, -4)$
C) $(4, -3)$
D) $(-3, 4)$

68. Last week, David slept 5 less hours than Gregory. If they slept a combined total of 99 hours, how many hours did Gregory sleep last week?

69. In 2012, Timothy had a collection consisting of 123 comic books. Starting in 2013, Timothy has been collecting 15 comic books per year. At this rate, in which year will Timothy first have had at least 141 comic books?

70. The line with the equation $\frac{2}{7}x + \frac{3}{5}y = 2$ is graphed in the xy-plane. What is the y-intercept of the line?

$$3x + y = 7$$
$$y = 2x - 1$$

71. In the solution (x, y) to the system of equations above, what is the value of y ?

72. The sum of two numbers is 50, and the difference when the smaller number is subtracted from the larger number is 10. What is the product of the two numbers?

LEVEL 3: PASSPORT TO ADVANCED MATH

$$f(x) = |2x - 3| - 1$$

73. For what positive value of x is $f(x)$ equal to 2 ?

   A) 0
   B) 2
   C) 3
   D) There is no such positive value of x.

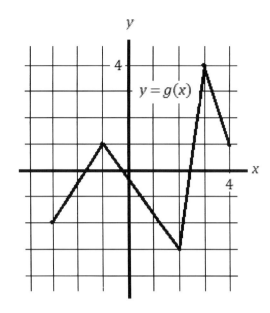

74. The entire graph of the function g is shown in the xy-plane above. Which of the following are equal to 7 ?

    I. $g(2) - g(3)$
  II. $g(3) - g(2)$
 III. $g(2) + g(3)$

    A) I only
    B) II only
    C) III only
    D) II, and III only

75. In the xy-plane, the graph of function g has x-intercepts at -3, -1, and 3. Which of the following could define g ?

    A) $g(x) = (x - 3)^2(x - 1)^2$
    B) $g(x) = (x + 3)^2(x + 1)^2$
    C) $g(x) = (x - 3)^2(x + 1)(x + 3)$
    D) $g(x) = (x - 3)(x + 3)(x - 1)^2$

76. For a positive real number k, where $k^5 = 3$, what is the value of k^{10} ?

    A) 27
    B) 9
    C) 6
    D) $\sqrt{10}$

77. If $\frac{2d-3c}{3c} = \frac{2}{5}$, which of the following must also be true?

    A) $\frac{c}{d} = \frac{21}{10}$

    B) $\frac{c}{d} = \frac{10}{21}$

    C) $\frac{2d+3c}{3c} = \frac{21}{10}$

    D) $\frac{2d}{3c} = \frac{5}{7}$

78. Ohm's law states that the current I through a conductor between two points is found by dividing the voltage V across the two points by the resistance R of the conductor. Which of the following equations gives the voltage V in terms of I and R ?

    A) $V = I + R$

    B) $V = IR$

    C) $V = \frac{I}{R}$

    D) $V = \frac{R}{I}$

$$x^2 + 5 = \frac{5}{x^2 + 5}$$

79. In the equation above, which of the following is a possible value of $x^2 + 5$?

    A) 25

    B) 5

    C) $\sqrt{5}$

    D) $5 - \sqrt{5}$

$$x - 3 = \sqrt{3x - b}$$

80. If $b = 5$, what is the solution set of the equation above?

    A) $\{2\}$

    B) $\{7\}$

    C) $\{2, 7\}$

    D) There are no solutions.

LEVEL 3: PROBLEM SOLVING

81. Laurie has three balls: a red ball, a blue ball, and a green ball. The weight of the red ball is approximately $\frac{11}{20}$ of the weight of the green ball, and the weight of the blue ball is approximately $\frac{27}{20}$ of the weight of the green ball. If the green ball weighs 30 pounds, approximately how many more pounds is the blue ball than the red ball?

   A) 16.5
   B) 24
   C) 31
   D) 40.4

x	1	2	3	4
y	$\frac{3}{2}$	$\frac{19}{6}$	$\frac{29}{6}$	$\frac{13}{2}$

82. Which of the following equations relates y to x for the values in the table above?

   A) $y = \frac{1}{6}x + \frac{4}{3}$
   B) $y = \frac{5}{3}x - \frac{1}{6}$
   C) $y = \frac{1}{3}\left(\frac{9}{2}\right)^x$
   D) $y = 3\left(\frac{1}{2}\right)^x$

Questions 83 - 86 refer to the following information.

Favorite Animals

	Dog	Cat	Elephant	Monkey	Lion	Total
Fresh	82	17	20	36	18	173
Soph	51	46	5	50	6	158
Jun	24	30	63	22	30	169
Total	157	93	88	108	54	500

The table above lists the results of a survey of a random sample of 500 high school freshman, sophomores, and juniors. Each student selected exactly one animal that was his or her favorite.

83. * If one of the freshman from the sample is selected at random, which of the following is closest to the percentage of students who selected the monkey as his or her favorite animal?

   A) 7%
   B) 21%
   C) 33%
   D) 50%

226

84. If one of the 500 students is selected at random, what is the probability that the student's favorite animal is an elephant or lion?

A) $\dfrac{11}{500}$

B) $\dfrac{27}{500}$

C) $\dfrac{93}{500}$

D) $\dfrac{71}{250}$

85. * If the sample is representative of a high school with 2,500 freshmen, sophomores and juniors, then based on the table, what is the predicted number of juniors at the high school who would select the elephant as their favorite animal?

A) 63

B) 88

C) 315

D) 845

Paramecia present (in thousands) over twelve days

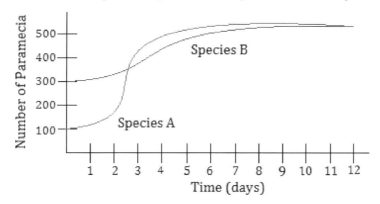

86. A small puddle is monitored by scientists for the number of *paramecia* present. The scientists are interested in two distinct species, let's call them "species *A*" and "species *B*." At time $t = 0$, the scientists measure and estimate the amount of species *A* and species *B* present in the puddle. They then proceed to measure and record the number of each species of *paramecium* present every hour for 12 days. The data for each species were then fit by a smooth curve, as shown in the graph above. Which of the following is a correct statement about the data above?

A) At time $t = 0$, the number of species *B* present is 150% greater than the number of species *A* present.

B) At time $t = 0$, the number of species *A* present is 75% less than the number of species *B* present.

C) For the first 3 days, the average growth rate of species *B* is higher than the average growth rate of species *A*.

D) The growth rate of both species *A* and species *B* decreases for the last 8 days.

87. The prom committee at a high school surveyed a random sample of 120 high school seniors to determine whether they should have an 80's or 90's themed prom. Of the students surveyed, 35% preferred to have a 90's themed prom. Based on this information, about how many students in the entire 300-person senior class would be expected to prefer having the prom with a 90's theme?

   A) 95
   B) 100
   C) 105
   D) 110

88. A group of colleagues plan to divide the $2400 cost of a business conference equally amongst themselves. When six of the colleagues decided not to attend the conference, those remaining still divided the $2400 cost equally, but each colleague's share of the cost increased by $90. How many colleagues were in the original group?

LEVEL 3: GEOMETRY AND COMPLEX NUMBERS

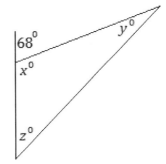

89. In the figure above, one side of a triangle is extended. Which of the following is true?

   A) $y = 68$
   B) $z = 68$
   C) $y + z = 68$
   D) $z - y = 68$

228

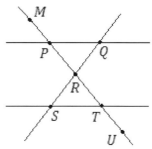

Note: Figure not drawn to scale.

90. In the figure above, $\angle MPQ \cong \angle STU$. Each of the following statements must be true EXCEPT

A) $\overline{PQ} \parallel \overline{ST}$
B) $m\angle MPQ + m\angle RTS = 180°$
C) $\Delta PQR \sim \Delta TSR$
D) $\Delta PQR \cong \Delta TSR$

91. If each side length of a rectangle is doubled, how would the area of the rectangle change?

A) The area would be multiplied by 4.
B) The area would be multiplied by 2.
C) The area would not change.
D) The area would be cut in half.

92. If $i = \sqrt{-1}$, which of the following complex numbers is equivalent to $(-7 - 3i)(5 - i)$?

A) $-35 + 3i$
B) $-35 - 3i$
C) $-32 - 8i$
D) $-38 - 8i$

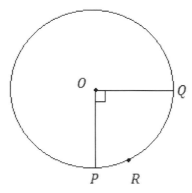

93. In the circle above with center O, $\angle POQ$ is a right angle. If the length of arc $\overset{\frown}{PRQ}$ is 10π, what is the length of a <u>diameter</u> of the circle?

94. * A heptagon is a polygon with 7 sides and 7 angles. What is the degree measure of an interior angle of a regular heptagon, to the nearest degree? (Disregard the degree symbol when gridding your answer.)

95. * A crystal shaped like a pyramid has a rectangular base such that the length of the base is $\frac{1}{3}$ the width of the base and the height is twice the length of the base. If the volume of the pyramid is 250 cubic inches, what is the height of the pyramid, in inches?

96. A circle with center $(1, 4)$ lies in the xy-plane. The circle has x-intercepts $(4, 0)$ and $(-2, 0)$. What is the radius of the circle?

LEVEL 4: HEART OF ALGEBRA

97. Joseph joins a gym that charges \$79.99 per month plus tax for a premium membership. A tax of 6% is applied to the monthly fee. Joseph is also charged a one-time initiation fee of \$95 as soon as he joins. There is no contract so that Joseph can cancel at any time without having to pay a penalty. Which of the following represents Joseph's total charge, in dollars, if he keeps his membership for t months?

   A) $1.06(79.99 + 95)t$
   B) $1.06(79.99t + 95)$
   C) $1.06(79.99t) + 95$
   D) $(79.99 + 0.06t) + 95$

98. The graph of $y = g(x)$ is a line in the xy-plane with slope 7. Given that $g(-8) = 11$, which of the following could be the definition of $g(x)$?

   A) $g(x) = 7x$
   B) $g(x) = 7x + 67$
   C) $g(x) = 7x - 67$
   D) $g(x) = 7x + 45$

$$2x + 5y = 3$$

99. The graph of the equation above is a line in the xy-plane. In which of the following equivalent forms of the equation does the y-intercept appear as a constant or coefficient?

   A) $5y = 3 - 2x$
   B) $x = \frac{3}{2} - \frac{5}{2}y$
   C) $y = \frac{3}{5} - \frac{2}{5}x$
   D) $2x - 5y - 3 = 0$

$$3x + y = 20$$
$$2x - 0.5y = 21.5$$

100. The solution to the system of equations above is (x, y). What is the value of y ?

    A) -7
    B) 5
    C) 9
    D) 63

101. A hospital manager will purchase first aid supplies and new machinery. The hospital has $75,000 left in its budget for the month. Each first aid kit costs the hospital $15 and each new piece of machinery costs the hospital $1200. Additionally, there is room for only 45 new pieces of machinery in the hospital. If k represents the number of first aid kits and m represents the number of pieces of machinery, which of the following systems of inequalities models this situation?

    A) $15k + 1200m \geq 75{,}000$
        $1 \leq k + m \leq 45$

    B) $15k + 1200m \geq 75{,}000$
        $1 \leq m \leq 45$
        $k \geq 1$

    C) $15k + 1200m \leq 75{,}000$
        $1 \leq k + m \leq 45$

    D) $15k + 1200m \leq 75{,}000$
        $1 \leq m \leq 45$
        $k \geq 1$

102. If $-\frac{27}{10} < 2 - 5x < -\frac{13}{5}$, then what is one possible value of $20x - 8$?

Cost of Coffee

Year	Price
1990	$0.15
1995	$0.28

103. The table above shows the price of coffee at a small coffee shop in Nebraska, for the years 1990 and 1995. If the relationship between coffee price and year is linear, which of the following functions C models the cost of coffee in dollars at this coffee shop t years after 1990 ?

    A) $C(t) = 0.15 + 0.026t$
    B) $C(t) = 0.15 + 0.26t$
    C) $C(t) = 0.15 + 0.026(t - 1990)$
    D) $C(t) = 0.15 + 0.26(t - 1990)$

104. A group of 51 people went on a canoeing excursion. A total of 23 canoes were used. Some of the canoes held 3 people, and the rest of the canoes held 2 people. Assuming all 23 of the canoes were filled to capacity and every person in the group participated in the excursion, exactly how many 3-person canoes were there?

LEVEL 4: PASSPORT TO ADVANCED MATH

105. Which of the following expressions is equivalent to $(9x^7y^5)^{\frac{1}{2}}$, for x and y nonnegative?

   A) $3x^{\frac{7}{2}}y^{\frac{5}{2}}$
   B) $3x^{\sqrt{7}}y^5$
   C) $\frac{9}{2}x^{\frac{7}{2}}y^5$
   D) $\frac{9}{2}x^{\sqrt{7}}y^{\frac{5}{2}}$

$$\frac{7}{x+3}+\frac{6}{3(x+3)}$$

106. Which of the following expressions is equivalent to the one above, where $x \neq -3$?

   A) $\frac{27}{3x+9}$
   B) $\frac{16}{3x+9}$
   C) $\frac{13}{x+3}$
   D) $\frac{9}{x+3}$

107. Which of the following is the set of x-values that are solutions to the quadratic equation $5x^2 + 15x - 50 = 0$?

   A) $\{-2,-5\}$
   B) $\{-2,5\}$
   C) $\{2,-5\}$
   D) $\{2,5\}$

108. What are the solutions to $x^2 - 5 = x$?

   A) $x = \frac{-1\pm\sqrt{29}}{2}$
   B) $x = \frac{-1\pm\sqrt{21}}{2}$
   C) $x = \frac{1\pm\sqrt{29}}{2}$
   D) $x = \frac{1\pm\sqrt{21}}{2}$

$$h(t) = -16t^2 + bt + c$$

109. In the function above, b and c are positive constants. The function models the height h, in feet, of an object above ground level t seconds after being thrown straight up in the air. What does the constant c represent in the function?

    A) The initial speed, in feet per second, of the object
    B) The maximum speed, in feet per second, of the object
    C) The initial height, in feet, of the object
    D) The maximum height, in feet, of the object

110. If $\frac{2k+3}{3k-1} = 2$, what is the value of k ?

111. If $5 + 4x^2 = 5x^2 - 9x + 25$, what is one possible value of x ?

112. If $(x + 3)^2 - 10(x + 3) + 25 = 0$, what is the value of x ?

LEVEL 4: PROBLEM SOLVING

113. 100 residents from a particular city were chosen at random and asked if they had pets. 45 of them reported that they did have pets. If the reported percentage is used as an estimate for the proportion of all residents in the town who have pets, the margin of error is 11%. Which of the following is the most appropriate conclusion based on the data provided?

    A) Between 0% and 34% of all the residents in the city have pets.
    B) Between 34% and 56% of all the residents of the city have pets.
    C) Approximately 33% of all the residents in the city have pets.
    D) 45% of all the residents in the city have pets.

Questions 114 - 117 refer to the following information.

The scatterplot below shows the number of people diagnosed with melanoma, in ten-thousands, from 1940 to 1970.

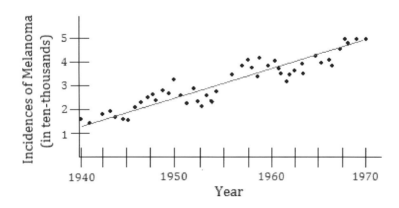

233

114. Based on the data shown in the figure, in 1969, approximately how many incidences of melanoma were there?

 A) 5
 B) 5000
 C) 40,000
 D) 50,000

115. According to the line of best fit, which of the following best approximates the year in which the number of incidences of melanoma was estimated to be 20,000 ?

 A) 1942
 B) 1946
 C) 1950
 D) 1954

116. Based on the line of best fit to the data, as shown in the figure, which of the following values is closest to the average yearly increase in the number of incidences of melanoma?

 A) 1,300
 B) 330
 C) 0.33
 D) 0.13

117. Based on the data shown in the figure, which of the following values is closest to the range of the number of incidences of melanoma between 1945 and 1950 ?

 A) 5,000
 B) 10,000
 C) 17,000
 D) 36,000

118. On January 1, 2015, a family living on an island releases their two pet rabbits into the wild. Due to the short gestation period of rabbits, and the fact that the rabbits have no natural predators on this island, the rabbit population doubles each month. If P represents the rabbit population t years after January 1, 2015, then which of the following equations best models the rabbit population on this island over time?

 A) $P = 2^{\frac{t+12}{12}}$
 B) $P = 2^{t+1}$
 C) $P = 2^{12t}$
 D) $P = 2^{12t+1}$

Questions 119 – 120 refer to the following information.

Fabric	Cost per square foot in US dollars	Cost per square foot in British pounds
Cotton	0.41	0.31
Wool	0.66	0.50
Silk	1.17	0.89

The table above gives the typical cost per square foot of several fabrics in both US dollars and British pounds on November 1, 2017.

119. * The ratio of the cost of cotton per square foot in British pounds to the cost of cotton per square foot in US dollars is b: 1, where b is a constant. What is the value of b, rounded to the nearest hundredth?

120. * What percent of the cost of silk in US dollars is the cost of wool in US dollars? (Disregard the percent symbol when gridding your answer.)

LEVEL 4: GEOMETRY AND COMPLEX NUMBERS

121. In ΔDOG, the measure of $\angle D$ is 60° and the measure of $\angle O$ is 30°. If $\overline{DO}$ is 8 units long, what is the area, in square units, of ΔDOG ?

A) 4
B) 8
C) $8\sqrt{2}$
D) $8\sqrt{3}$

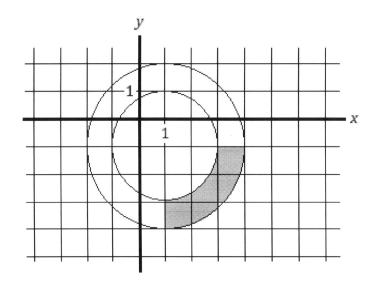

122. Two circles are drawn in the xy-plane above. Both circles have center $(1, -1)$ and their diameters are 4 and 6, respectively. What is the area of the shaded region?

A) $\frac{5\pi}{4}$

B) $\frac{5\pi}{2}$

C) $\frac{25\pi}{8}$

D) 5π

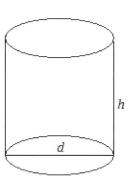

$$SA = 2\pi(\frac{d}{2})^2 + \pi dh$$

123. The formula above can be used to calculate the total surface area of the right circular cylinder shown, where h is the height of the cylinder, and d is the diameter of each circular base. What must the expression πdh represent?

A) The area of a circular base
B) The sum of the areas of the two circular bases
C) The lateral surface area
D) The sum of the area of one circular base and the lateral surface area

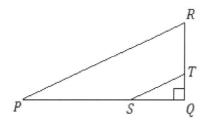

124. In the figure above, $\overline{ST} \parallel \overline{PR}$, $PS = 5$ and $SQ = 2$. What is the ratio of the length of segment $\overline{ST}$ to the length of segment $\overline{PR}$?

   A) $2:5$
   B) $2:6$
   C) $2:7$
   D) $3:7$

125. If the side length of a rhombus is doubled, how would the area of the rhombus change?

   A) The area would be multiplied by 4.
   B) The area would be multiplied by 2.
   C) The area would not change.
   D) The area would be cut in half.

126. Acute angles A and B satisfy $\sin A = \cos B$. If $m\angle A = (3d - 5)°$ and $m\angle B = (2d - 7)°$, what is the value of d ?

127. A line segment is drawn from the center of a 15-sided regular polygon to each vertex of the polygon forming 15 isosceles triangles. What is the measure of a base angle of one of these triangles? (Disregard the degree symbol when gridding your answer.)

128. * If $i = \sqrt{-1}$, and $\frac{(2-3i)}{(i-7)} = a + bi$, where a and b are real numbers, then what is the value of $|a|$ to the nearest tenth?

LEVEL 5: HEART OF ALGEBRA

129. A paleontologist estimates the weight of a new dinosaur species to be w tons, where $w > 20$. For an experiment to be successful, the paleontologist needs his estimate to be within 2 tons of the actual weight of the dinosaur. If the experiment is successful and the actual weight of the dinosaur is z tons, which of the following inequalities gives the relationship between the actual weight of the dinosaur and the paleontologist's estimate?

   A) $w > z + 2$
   B) $z > w + 2$
   C) $w - z < 2$
   D) $-2 < z - w < 2$

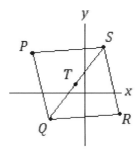

Note: Figure not drawn to scale.

130. In the xy-plane above, point T is the center of the square $PQRS$. The coordinates of points S and T are $(2, 5)$ and $(-1, 1)$, respectively. Which of the following is an equation of the line that passes through points P and R ?

   A) $y = 1$

   B) $y = -\frac{3}{4}x + 1$

   C) $y = \frac{3}{4}x - \frac{1}{4}$

   D) $y = -\frac{3}{4}x + \frac{1}{4}$

131. If $15 - 5x < -7$, which inequality represents the possible range of values of $6x - 18$?

   A) $\frac{42}{5} < 6x - 18$

   B) $\frac{42}{5} > 6x - 18$

   C) $\frac{32}{5} < 6x - 18$

   D) $\frac{32}{5} > 6x - 18$

132. An x% saline solution is a mixture of salt and water consisting of x% salt. Jessie wants to make a mixture of no more than 5 quarts from a 3% solution, a 7% solution, and a 12% solution to get a solution consisting of at least 10% salt. Let x be the number of quarts of the 3% solution, let y be the number of quarts of the 7% solution, and let z be the number of quarts of the 12% solution in the mixture. Which of the following systems represents all the constraints that x, y, and z must satisfy?

A) $\begin{cases} 0 < x < 5 \\ 0 < y < 5 \\ 0 < z < 5 \\ \frac{3x+7y+12z}{x+y+z} \geq 10 \end{cases}$

B) $\begin{cases} x > 0 \\ y > 0 \\ z > 0 \\ x + y + z \leq 5 \\ 3x + 7y + 12z \geq 10(x + y + z) \end{cases}$

C) $\begin{cases} x > 0 \\ y > 0 \\ z > 0 \\ x + y + z \leq 5 \\ 3x + 7y + 12z \geq 10 \end{cases}$

D) $\begin{cases} x > 0 \\ y > 0 \\ z > 0 \\ x + y + z = 5 \\ 3x + 7y + 12z \leq 10 \end{cases}$

$$x + 3y \geq -3$$
$$5x - 7y \leq 35$$

133. In the xy-plane, if a point with coordinates (a, b) lies in the solution set of the system of inequalities above, what is the maximum possible value of b?

A) $-\dfrac{25}{11}$

B) $\dfrac{25}{11}$

C) $\dfrac{42}{11}$

D) There is no maximum value for b.

x	$L(x)$
-3	8
1	16
5	24

134. Some values of the linear function L are shown in the table above. What is $L(-2)$?

$$4x = 3y - 1$$
$$7y = 5x + 3$$

135. (a, b) are the coordinates of the point of intersection of the two lines in the plane that are the graphs of the equations given above. What is the value of b ?

$$ax - 5y = c$$
$$3x + by = 7$$

136. In the system of equations above, a, b, and c are constants. If the two equations represent the same line, what is the value of ab^2c ?

LEVEL 5: PASSPORT TO ADVANCED MATH

137. For a polynomial $g(x)$, the value of $g(-3)$ is 2. Which of the following must be true about $g(x)$?

   A) $x - 5$ is a factor of $g(x)$.
   B) $x - 2$ is a factor of $g(x)$.
   C) The remainder when $g(x)$ is divided by $x + 3$ is 2.
   D) The remainder when $g(x)$ is divided by $x - 3$ is 2.

138. Which of the following is an equivalent form of $\sqrt[4]{x^{12m}y^3}$, where x and y are both positive?

   A) $x^{3m}y^{\frac{3}{4}}$
   B) $x^{4m}y^{-1}$
   C) $x^{\frac{1}{2m}}y^{\frac{4}{3}}$
   D) $x^{\frac{1}{3m}}y^{-1}$

$$h(x) = (x - 3)(x + 7)$$

139. Which of the following is an equivalent form of the function h above in which the minimum value of h appears as a coefficient or constant?

   A) $h(x) = x^2 - 21$
   B) $h(x) = x^2 + 4x - 21$
   C) $h(x) = (x - 2)^2 - 21$
   D) $h(x) = (x + 2)^2 - 25$

140. Let $f(x) = \frac{1}{3}(x-3)^2 + 2$ and $g(x) = 3x - 13$. What is one possible value of c such that $f(c) = g(c)$?

141. If the expression $\frac{x^3 - 5x^2 + 3x + 9}{x-1}$ is written in the equivalent form $ax^2 + bx + c + \frac{d}{x-1}$, what is the value of d ?

142. The expression $|3 - 8x| > 34$ is equivalent to $x < a$ or $x > b$. What is the value of $b - a$?

$$f(x) = 2x^2 - 18x + 12$$

143. Let a be the product of the roots of the function f shown above, and let b be the sum of the roots of f. What is the value of $\frac{a}{b}$?

$$2x^2 - y^2 = 16$$
$$2x - y = 4$$

144. If (x, y) is a solution to the system of equations above, what is the value of x ?

LEVEL 5: PROBLEM SOLVING

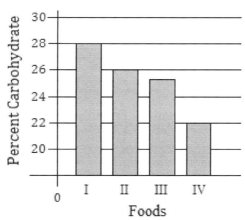

Percent Carbohydrate in Four Foods

145. * The graph above shows the amount of carbohydrate supplied by four different foods, I, II, III, and IV, as a percentage of their total weights. The cost of 20 ounces of foods I, II, III, and IV, are \$4.00, \$3.50, \$3.00, and \$2.75, respectively. Which of the four foods supplies the most carbohydrate per dollar?

A) I
B) II
C) III
D) IV

146. Suppose that the average (arithmetic mean) of a, b, and c is h, the average of b, c, and d is j, and the average of d and e is k. What is the average of a and e ?

    A) $h - j + k$

    B) $\dfrac{3h + 3j - 2k}{2}$

    C) $\dfrac{3h - 3j + 2k}{2}$

    D) $\dfrac{3h - 3j + 2k}{5}$

147. To determine if exercising regularly reduces the risk of diabetes in women, scientists interviewed a random sample of 8,000 women who had no family history of diabetes. Participants in the study were identified as occasional or regular exercisers. Ten years later, the scientists found that the proportion of women with diabetes was significantly lower for the women identified as regular exercisers. Which of the following is the most reasonable conclusion?

    A) Exercising regularly reduces the risk of diabetes in women, but not necessarily in men.
    B) Exercising regularly reduces the risk of diabetes in both women and men.
    C) There is an association between exercising regularly and the risk of diabetes for women, but it is not necessarily a cause-and-effect relationship, and the association may not exist for men.
    D) There is an association between exercising regularly and the risk of diabetes for women and men, but it is not necessarily a cause-and-effect relationship.

148. A rectangle was changed by increasing its length by r percent and decreasing its width by 20%. If these changes increased the area of the rectangle by 4%, what is the value of r ?

    A) 10
    B) 20
    C) 30
    D) 40

149. * A survey was conducted among a randomly chosen sample of 250 single men and 250 single women about whether they owned any dogs or cats. The table below displays a summary of the survey results.

	Dogs Only	Cats Only	Both	Neither	Total
Men	92	27	5	126	250
Women	75	43	34	98	250
Total	167	70	39	224	500

According to the table, which of the following statements is most likely to be false?

A) The probability that a woman is a cat owner is greater than the probability that a cat owner is a woman

B) The probability that a dog owner is male is greater than the probability that a randomly chosen person is a cat owner.

C) The probability that a woman does not own a dog or cat is greater than the probability that a man owns at least one dog and one cat.

D) The probability that a cat owner is a woman is greater than the probability that a man owns a dog.

$$S = 161{,}400 \left(1 + \frac{16.9}{100}\right)^t$$

150. The mean annual salary of an NBA player, S, can be estimated using the equation above, where S is measured in thousands of dollars, and t represents the number of years since 1980 for $0 \le t \le 20$. Which of the following statements is the best interpretation of 16.9 in the context of this problem?

A) The estimated mean annual salary, in dollars, of an NBA player in 1980.
B) The estimated mean annual salary, in dollars, of an NBA player in 2000.
C) The estimated yearly increase in the mean annual salary of an NBA player.
D) The estimated yearly percent increase in the mean annual salary of an NBA player.

Questions 151 - 152 refer to the following information.

A biologist places a colony consisting of 5000 bacteria into a petri dish. After the initial placement of the bacteria at time $t = 0$, the biologist measures and estimates the number of bacteria present every half hour. This data was then fitted by an exponential curve of the form $y = c \cdot 2^{kt}$ where c and k are constants, t is measured in hours, and y is measured in thousands of bacteria. The scatterplot together with the exponential curve are shown below.

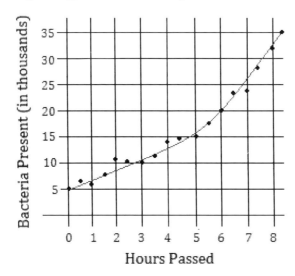

151. According to the scatterplot, the biologist's measurements indicate that the number of bacteria present quadrupled in 6 hours, and the exponential curve passes through the corresponding data point at time $t = 6$. The exponential function also agrees with the initial number of bacteria. What is the value of ck ?

152. Suppose that the data was fitted with a quadratic function of the form $t^2 + bt + c$ instead of an exponential function. Assume that the quadratic function agrees with the scatterplot at times $t = 0$ and $t = 6$. What is the t-coordinate of the vertex of the graph of the quadratic function?

LEVEL 5: GEOMETRY AND COMPLEX NUMBERS

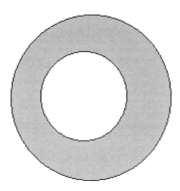

153. A circular disk is cut out of a larger circular disk, as shown in the figure above, so that the area of the piece that remains is the same as the area of the cutout. If the radius of the larger circle is R, what is the circumference of the cutout, in terms of R ?

    A) $R\pi$
    B) $R\sqrt{2}$
    C) $R\pi\sqrt{2}$
    D) $2R\pi\sqrt{2}$

154. A right circular cylinder has a base diameter of 4 and height 7. If point O is the center of the top of the cylinder and B lies on the circumference of the bottom of the cylinder, what is the straight-line distance between O and B ?

    A) 3
    B) 7
    C) 11
    D) $\sqrt{53}$

155. * Jonathon wants to place a rectangular fence around the border to his backyard. The width of the fence will be 350 inches more than 5 times the length of the fence. What will be the perimeter of Jonathon's fence if the area of the fence is 64,680 square inches?

    A) 854 inches
    B) 1274 inches
    C) 1708 inches
    D) 2548 inches

156. It is given that $\cos x = k$, where x is the radian measure of an angle and $\pi < x < \frac{3\pi}{2}$. If $\cos z = -k$, which of the following could <u>not</u> be the value of z ?

    A) $x - \pi$
    B) $\pi - x$
    C) $2\pi - x$
    D) $3\pi - x$

157. Let $i = \sqrt{-1}$, $z = a + bi$, and $\overline{z} = a - bi$. We define the absolute value of z to be $|z| = \sqrt{z\overline{z}}$. Which of the following is true?

    A) $|z|$ is always a nonnegative real number.
    B) $|z|$ is always a real number that can be positive, negative, or zero.
    C) $|z|$ is never a real number.
    D) $|z|$ can be real or complex.

158. A rectangular prism has a length that is 4 centimeters less than its height, and a width that is 4 centimeters more than its height. If the volume of the prism is 120 cubic centimeters, what is the surface area of the prism, in square centimeters?

$$\cos x = \sin(c - x)$$

159. In the equation above, $0 \leq c < 2\pi$. If c and x are given in radians, what is one possible value of c, to the nearest tenth?

160. * The graph of $x^2 - 7x + y^2 - 13y - 14 = 0$ in the xy-plane is a circle. To the nearest tenth, what is the radius of the circle?

UNI SAYS...

The Challenge Problems on the following page are NOT SAT questions. However, working out the solutions to these problems WILL increase your level of mathematical maturity. If you are trying to get a perfect score in SAT math, but cannot seem to get past the low to mid 700's, then a boost in your mathematical skill level may be exactly what you need to break through this final sticking point. Make sure to spend some time struggling with each problem before checking the solution. It is the struggle that will make your mind stronger. Best of luck!

Full solutions to the Challenge Problems are available for free download here:
www.SATPrepGet800.com/UniSATxWB

CHALLENGE PROBLEMS

1. If x and y are positive real numbers with $x^8 = \frac{z^3}{16}$ and $x^{12} = \frac{z^7}{y^4}$, what is the value of $\frac{xy}{z}$?

2. If $2x + 3y - 4z = 2$, $x - y + 5z = 6$ and $3x + 2y - z = 4$, what is the value of y ?

3. The graphs of $y = bx^2$ and $y = k - bx^2$ intersect at points A and B. If the length of $\overline{AB}$ is equal to d, what is the value of $\frac{bd^2}{k}$?

4. Let the function h be defined by $h(x) = x^3 + 12$. If c is a positive number such that $h(c^2) = h(3d)$ and $d = \sqrt{c}$, what is the value of $c^{\frac{3}{2}}$?

5. Let f and g be functions such that $f(x) = ax^2 + bx + c$ and $g(x) = ax + b$. If $g(1) = 2b - a + 25$ and $g(2) = 2a - 24$, then for what value of x does $f(x) = f(8)$, where $x \neq 8$?

6. Show that $x^2 + y^2 + z^2 \geq xy + yz + zx$ for positive numbers x, y, and z.

7. Use the method of completing the square to derive the quadratic formula.

8. Suppose that quadrilateral $PQRS$ has four congruent sides and satisfies $PQ = PR$. What is the value of $\frac{QS}{PR}$?

9. Draw a rectangular solid with sides of length a, b and c, and let the long diagonal have length d. Show geometrically that $d^2 = a^2 + b^2 + c^2$.

10. A cube is inscribed in a cone of radius 1 and height 2 so that one face of the cube is contained in the base of the cone. What is the length of a side of the cube?

11. If 2 real numbers are randomly chosen from a line segment of length 10, what is the probability that the distance between them is at least 7 ?

12. Show that if x is the least integer in a set of $n + 1$ consecutive integers, then the median of the set is $x + \frac{n}{2}$.

13. Show that in a set of consecutive integers, the average (arithmetic mean) and median are equal.

14. B is a **subset** of a set A if every element of B is an element of A. For example, if $A = \{a, b\}$, then all the subsets of A are $\emptyset$, $\{a\}$, $\{b\}$, and A (here $\emptyset$ is the **emptyset**, the unique set consisting of no elements). How many subsets does the set $\{1, 2, \dots, n\}$ have where n is a positive integer?

15. Define a set to be **selfish** if the number of elements it has is in the set. For example, $X_{10} = \{1, 2, 3, 4, 5, 6, 7, 8, 9, 10\}$ is selfish because it has 10 elements, and 10 is in the set. How many selfish subsets does X_n have, where n is a positive integer?

16. A selfish set is **minimal** if none of its proper subsets is also selfish. For example, the set X_{10} is not a minimal selfish set because $\{1\}$ is a selfish subset. Let $X_n = \{1, \dots, n\}$. In terms of n, how many minimal selfish subsets does the set X_n have?

ACTIONS TO COMPLETE AFTER YOU HAVE READ THIS BOOK

1. Take another practice SAT

You should see a substantial improvement in your score.

2. Continue to practice SAT math problems for 10 to 20 minutes each day

You may want to purchase *320 SAT Math Problems arranged by Topic and Difficulty Level* for additional practice problems.

3. 'Like' my Facebook page

This page is updated regularly with SAT prep advice, tips, tricks, strategies, and practice problems. Visit the following webpage and click the 'like' button.

www.facebook.com/SATPrepGet800

4. Review this book

If this book helped you, please post your positive feedback on the site you purchased it from; e.g. Amazon, Barnes and Noble, etc.

5. Claim your FREE bonuses

If you have not done so yet, visit the following webpage and enter your email address to receive solutions to all the problems in this book and other materials.

www.SATPrepGet800.com/UniSATxWB

About the Author

Dr. Steve Warner, a New York native, earned his Ph.D. at Rutgers University in Pure Mathematics in May 2001. While a graduate student, Dr. Warner won the TA Teaching Excellence Award.

After Rutgers, Dr. Warner joined the Penn State Mathematics Department as an Assistant Professor. In September 2002, Dr. Warner returned to New York to accept an Assistant Professor position at Hofstra University. By September 2007, Dr. Warner had received tenure and was promoted to Associate Professor. He has taught undergraduate and graduate courses in Precalculus, Calculus, Linear Algebra, Differential Equations, Mathematical Logic, Set Theory and Abstract Algebra.

Over that time, Dr. Warner participated in a five-year NSF grant, "The MSTP Project," to study and improve mathematics and science curriculum in poorly performing junior high schools. He also published several articles in scholarly journals, specifically on Mathematical Logic.

Dr. Warner has more than 15 years of experience in general math tutoring and tutoring for standardized tests such as the SAT, ACT and AP Calculus exams. He has tutored students both individually and in group settings.

In February 2010 Dr. Warner released his first SAT prep book "The 32 Most Effective SAT Math Strategies," and in 2012 founded Get 800 Test Prep. Since then Dr. Warner has written books for the SAT, ACT, SAT Math Subject Tests, AP Calculus exams, and GRE.

Dr. Steve Warner can be reached at

steve@SATPrepGet800.com

BOOKS BY DR. STEVE WARNER

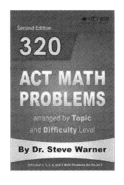   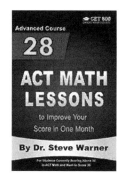

  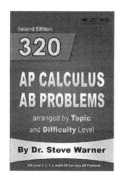 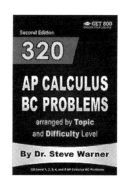

Made in the USA
San Bernardino, CA
27 July 2018